# The Weiser Field Guide to
# ascension

## The Meaning of Miracles and Shifts in Consciousness Past and Present

Cal Garrison

WEISER BOOKS
San Francisco, CA / Newburyport, MA

7-14

First published in 2010 by
Red Wheel/Weiser, LLC
With offices at:
500 Third Street, Suite 230
San Francisco, CA 94107
*www.redwheelweiser.com*

Library of Congress Cataloging-in-Publication Data
Garrison, Cal.
The Weiser field guide to ascension : the meaning of miracles and shifts in
consciousness past and present / Cal Garrison.
p. cm.
Includes bibliographical references.
ISBN 978-1-57863-469-9
1. Ascension of the soul. 2. Two thousand twelve, A.D. I. Title. II. Title: Field
guide to ascension.
BF1999.G34 2010
130—dc22
2009053007

Cover: pyramid, papyrus, meditation and energy photographs © dreamstime.com.
Jesus ascending, and out of body photographs © istockphoto.com.
Illustration of woman ascending © Miss Mary. Interior: images on pages 16, 19,
27, 28, 33, 35, 37, 38, 44, 55, 67, 69, 78, 82, 83, 97, 107, 123, 134, 144, 152, 162,
170, 178 © dreamstime.com. Images on pages 89, 111, 120, 200 © Miss Mary.
Image on page 151 © istockphoto.com. Images on pages 30 and
101 © Dover Publications.
Production Editor: Michele Kimble
Copy Editor: Tania Seymour
Proofreader: Nancy Reinhardt
Typeset in Jenson and Priori

Printed in Canada.
TCP
10  9  8  7  6  5  4  3  2  1
The paper used in this publication meets the minimum requirements of the
American National Standard for Information Sciences—Permanence of Paper for
Printed Library Materials Z39.48-1992 (R1997).

*To the Hundredth Monkey and the Light*
*that lives in all of us*

# Contents

# Introduction

When Weiser invited me to write this book, their instructions were to do an overview of the ascension phenomenon and explore the cultural myths that have grown up around both it and the Apocalypse. This would have been interesting—and it would have made sense—were it not for the fact that at approximately the same time more than one hundred Indigenous Elders from all over the world were gathered together in northern Arizona, performing ceremonies that were meant to prepare Mother Earth for her entrance into the Fifth World. With the Ancestors already drumming their prayers into the ground, it became obvious to me that we were so close to the point of ascension it would serve no purpose to talk about it from a purely intellectual perspective.

If we've made any attempt to examine the facts, chances are we understand that the Apocalypse is only one aspect of a much bigger phenomenon. Behind all the signs that point to doom and disaster, those of us who have heard about the ascension know that its mysteries are somehow connected to the 2012 scenario, but when we try to figure out how global catastrophe translates into a spiritual awakening, it becomes difficult to bridge the gap. As we consider possibilities and wonder what to expect, no matter who we are, the imminence of a dimensional shift begs us to explore the physics of the ascension process in a little more detail.

Unfortunately, the details are few and far between. Although much has been said about the metaphysics of the process, there isn't a whole lot to go on when it comes to hard facts and practical information. At the same time, the ones who have come forward with their stories and prophecies have shared enough to give us a clearer picture of how it works. Up until now, they have told us that our passage through the ascension portal will see us awakening to a whole new life in one of the most beautiful worlds in Creation. Only lately have they begun to more fully explain the actual mechanics of the process.

As much as I wish I could cover every last detail, what I know is limited to what the Elders have revealed so far. Until those secrets are disclosed in their entirety, consider this field guide to be a rough map to an unknown territory, and know that it was written to help you understand how what is ultimately a spiritual experience plays out at the physical level—because we are no longer in a position to be wondering about it. The Elders are clear when they tell us *The time has come.* We are about to be part of an event that takes place only every twenty-six thousand years. As we stand at the tipping point, contemplating the reality of the ascension process, knowing how it goes would seem to be more important than anything else.

If these words bring you to a deeper understanding of what we are about to go through, know that it was a privilege to write them—and if you grow as much from reading them as I did from committing them to paper, I know in my heart that the world will be better for it.

With Love,

Cal Garrison
Sedona, Arizona
September 9, 2009

## CHAPTER 1

# The Biblical Ascension

# Easter
## Reflections

My time in Sunday school was limited to an annual blossoming of spiritual fervor that only affected my family on Easter. Every now and then, we'd get dressed up and appear in church on other occasions, but there was no routine when it came to Sunday school. I'm not sure if that was because my parents wanted to sleep late or if it had something to do with the fact that we were Unitarian.

As most of you know, Unitarians don't have a lot of fixed ideas about God or any hard-and-fast rules regarding what people choose to do with their Sundays. Unlike my Catholic friends, I never had to read the Bible, didn't go to confirmation class, and had no idea what Holy Communion was all about. While Mary Elizabeth and Ann Marie got washed and ironed and herded off to Mass, I got to hang around in my pj's and

watch cartoons on Sunday mornings. Seen in retrospect, having no dogma to screw up my relationship with the divine was probably one of my luckier spiritual breaks, but at the time, not being in on any of their orthodox religious secrets made me feel totally out of it. Only once a year, on Easter, did I get to be one of them.

On that day, Heaven opened up for me. Between my Easter bonnet and my Easter basket, my black patent leather shoes and my little white gloves, this event was so huge that by the time I got to church, I was bursting with the desire to know what happened to Jesus. With one day to figure it all out, my focus was so intense, every word that came out of the minister's mouth regarding Christ's resurrection and his ascension echoed from the pulpit, reverberated off the walls, and lodged itself permanently in my little brain. It wasn't just his words; it was the hymns. The same story and the same awe-inspiring hymns, repeated year after year and received in a feeling state that was vibrating at a fever pitch; these things combined like some weird form of subliminal programming to carve an indelible series of images that deepened every Easter.

As I sit down to write this field guide to ascension, it amuses me that the one and only thing I picked up from going to church is what I have to write about. Little did I know that my Easter intensives were meant to prepare me for this. If my early visions of Christ vanishing into a cloud and rising bodily into the heavens form the foundation for what we are about to discuss, we might as well start this conversation by looking at what the Bible tells us about the Ascension.

Since most of us haven't had to consider the finer points of Christian dogma for quite some time, we'll have to talk about the crucifixion, the resurrection, and the Pentecost as well, because those three events appear to be intimately entwined with Christ's ascent into heaven.

# The Crucifixion, the Resurrection, the Ascension, and the Pentecost

After the crucifixion, out of respect for Jewish custom, Pontius Pilate gave Joseph of Arimathea and Nicodemus permission to take the body of Christ down from the Cross and place it in a tomb. Afraid that one of the faithful might come along and steal it, Pilate ordered a hundred Jewish guards to keep an eye on things at the sepulcher, just to make sure that the corpse stayed put.

FRED. CYDE. SC.

Early the following morning, Mary Magdalene went to the tomb and found the guards milling around in a state of confusion with no way to explain why the stone at the entrance had been moved or why the body of Christ was gone. Thinking that the corpse had been stolen, Mary ran to Simon and Peter and told them, *"They have taken the Lord out of the tomb and we don't know where they have put him."*[1]

Hearing this, Simon and Peter went to the tomb and found the situation to be exactly as Mary had described it: Christ's body was gone, his funeral shroud was lying on the ground, and the cloth that had covered his face was folded neatly next to the shroud. Forgetting that prior to his crucifixion their Master had told them that he would rise from the dead, the full import of the missing corpse was lost on all three of them. The story goes that the two men went home, while Mary Magdalene stood weeping outside the entrance to the tomb.

As she wept she stooped to look into the tomb and:

She beheld two angels in white sitting, one at the head, and one at the feet, where the body of Jesus had been lying. And they said to her, "Woman, why are you weeping?" She said to them, "Because they have taken away my Lord, and I do not know where they have laid him." When she had said this, she turned

around, and beheld Jesus standing there and
did not know that it was Jesus. Jesus said to her,
"Woman, why are you weeping?" Supposing
him to be the gardener, she said to him, "Sir,
if you have carried Him away, tell me where
you have laid Him and I will take Him away."
Jesus said to her, "Mary!" She turned and said
to Him in Hebrew, "Rabbouni!" (which means
Teacher). Jesus said to her, "Stop clinging to
Me, for I have not yet ascended to the Father:
but go to My brethren, and say to them, I
ascend to My Father and your Father, and My
God and your God." Mary Magdalene came,
announcing to the disciples, "I have seen the
Lord," and that he had said these things to her.[2]

The above passage tells us that Christ has risen
and that Mary Magdalene is the first of his disciples to
become aware of the fact that he has kept his promise to
return from the dead. After they recognize each other he
says, *Stop clinging to Me, for I have not yet ascended to the*
*Father.* For the next forty days, Christ appeared to the
apostles alive and in the flesh on numerous occasions:

To these He also presented himself alive, after
His suffering, by many convincing proofs, appearing
to them over a period of forty days, and speaking of
the things concerning the kingdom of God. And
gathering them together, He commanded them not
to leave Jerusalem, but to wait for what the Father

had promised. "*Which,*" He said, "*you heard of from Me; for John baptized with water, but you shall be baptized with the Holy Spirit not many days from now.*"[3]

Each time he appeared, Christ promised the disciples that something even more miraculous than his resurrection had yet to happen. When the time came for him to ascend, he gathered the apostles and:

> when they had come together, they were asking Him, saying, "Lord, is it at this time that You are restoring the kingdom to Israel?" He said to them, "It is not for you to know times or epochs which the Father has fixed by his own authority; but you shall receive power when the Holy Spirit has come upon you; and you shall be My witnesses both in Jerusalem, and in all Judea and Samaria, and even to the remotest part of the earth."
>
> And after He had said these things, He was lifted up while they were looking on, and a cloud received Him out of their sight. And as they were gazing intently into the sky while He was departing, behold, two men in white clothing stood beside them: and they also said, "Men of Galilee, why do you stand looking up into the sky? This Jesus, who has been taken up from you into heaven, will come in just the same way as you have watched Him go into heaven."[4]

The biblical authors must have decided to keep it simple when they wrote about Christ's ultimate miracle; either that, or the ascension story got heavily edited when the Council of Nicaea deleted so much of the original work. Two sentences of page space leave us with a bare bones description of Christ vanishing into a cloud. That's it. They barely finish telling us about it before they move right along to the words of the men in white, and the idea that one more miracle is about to manifest.

Since there's no way to squeeze any more information about the ascension out of what's written here, we have no choice but to see if the promise of another miracle sheds more light on the matter. According to the men in white, Christ was due to return in the same way he left and, sure enough, ten days after he ascended into heaven, Christ descended into matter in the form of the Holy Spirit, to teach yet another important lesson:

> And when the day of Pentecost had come, they were all together in one place. And suddenly there came from heaven a noise, like a violent, rushing wind, and it filled the whole house where they were sitting. And there appeared to them tongues as of fire distributing themselves, and they rested on each one of them. And they were all filled with the Holy Spirit and began to speak with other tongues, as the Spirit was giving them utterance.[5]

## Lost in Translation

So what does all of this mean? Do we dare to analyze it? I ask that question because for the past two thousand years, Christ's followers have gone crazy trying to figure out what his three most mind-blowing miracles were really all about. Unfortunately, the Bible is worded in a way that doesn't make it very clear. In addition to that, the good book has been rewritten and translated so many times, there are more than eight hundred versions of the same story. If that isn't enough to confuse us, the fact that the Council of Nicaea removed so much of the original text means that what we take to be the last word on everything is in reality the skeletal remains of the truth.

With that in mind, the standard take on the crucifixion and the resurrection has always been wrapped up in the idea that somehow or other, in getting nailed to the cross, Christ sacrificed himself and died for our sins. I don't know about you, but even as a kid, that idea never made much sense to me. First of all, what point would it make for him to die for our sins? Would humanity learn anything from this? Or would it just give us a perfect excuse to keep sinning away, under the illusion that the crucifixion made it all okay? Common sense tells me that this would only serve to perpetuate our troubles—and evidently it has; more than two thousand years later, we are no better off spiritually than we were on the day Christ was crucified.

Time and time again Jesus reminded us, "*What I do all men can do*." I am pretty sure he wasn't kidding. Everything Christ did was meant to teach us about the full extent of our connection to Spirit and to help us evolve into the fullest realization of the potentialities inherent in the archetype "Man." Each time he made an appearance, this was done, not to glorify his own remarkable abilities, but to demonstrate to all mankind that for anyone who has been awakened to Christ Consciousness, life can never be extinguished. An apparent miracle, his resurrection could just as easily be seen as a "live demonstration," one that was meant to show us that all of us are capable of the same thing.

His ascension took the lesson one step further. If, in resurrecting himself, Christ proved that it is possible to come back from the dead, his ascension showed us that for anyone who follows his example, it is also possible to leave this world and ascend to the higher levels without having to discard the physical body in the process. All of us have the inherent capacity to do this, but it is a birthright that only comes to life if we develop the Christed being within ourselves.

When it comes to the Pentecost, the different takes on what actually happened when the tongues of fire touched the hearts of the faithful have divided the Christian Church for centuries. I won't pretend to have it all figured out, but it seems to me that the descent of the Holy Spirit was another part of the same lesson. If his ascension taught us that the stairway to heaven goes up, the baptism of the Holy Spirit showed us, quite simply, that it goes both ways; spirit can ascend, but it can also descend into matter and shine as brightly here in the material world as it does in the higher realms.

Ultimately, the resurrection, the ascension, and the events of the Pentecost were all part of one lesson—a lesson that was meant to teach us about our own inherent abilities. *"What I do all men can do."* If we take Christ at his word, the miraculous things we attribute to him and the level of consciousness he developed in order to perform those miracles exist as potential in all of us. Underneath it all, Christ was trying to show us that the Holy Spirit lives inside each and every one of us and our purpose for living has to do with developing that aspect of ourselves as fully and completely as we can—which gets us to the heart of the matter.

Why did Christ go to such great lengths to teach us these things? What did we learn from him? Did those lessons inspire us to follow his example? And aside from what the Bible tells us, why do you suppose he went through all that just to inform us that we could do it too? And if we can do it too, why, after two thousand years of Christianity, are we still killing each other off in the name of the man who popped in for thirty-three years just to remind us that we have better things to do?

"*What I do all men can do.*" Christ meant what he said—but the Bible doesn't expand on that concept, nor does it come with a workable set of instructions. Fragments of teachings and words spoken long ago only reveal so much. With most of the pieces missing, there's no way to get the whole picture without leaning too heavily on conjecture—and conjecture rarely, if ever, adds up to the truth.

It wasn't until I outgrew my patent leather shoes and gave up on my Easter intensives that I found out that Christ didn't have a monopoly on the ascension process any more than the Christian Church had a monopoly on spirituality. This discovery totally blew me away, but it was the sixties, and everything was getting blown away. Between the psychedelic explosion and the New Age Movement, much of what we learned in church got displaced by ideas that came from other belief systems. Taoism, Buddhism, Theosophy, Tantra, Gnosticism, Rosicrucianism, Wicca, Yoga, the ancient Egyptian and Atlantean wisdom; you name it—old and new bodies of knowledge came out of the woodwork, opening the space for more light to shine on what the Bible didn't tell us.

In conjunction with this expansion of spiritual awareness, something else began to happen. It was around that time that the term "ascension" started coming up more and more in conversation, not in reference to the Christ story but in reference to some miraculous, mysterious process that humanity was about to go through. Up until the mid-1960s, Easter Sunday was the one and only day of the year that the word "ascension" even came up—but the minute it came to be associated with the Great Shift of the Ages, or the point in the Grand Cycle when the Precession of the Equinox would open the portal to the Aquarian Age, the term was on everyone's lips, begging for a clear definition.

Framed in a new light, the concept challenged too many core beliefs for anyone, including me, to fully comprehend it at the time; but ascension was such a hot topic, this lack of understanding gave rise to hundreds of ascension books. Various authors took it upon themselves to explain the process and its relationship to the times we're in. In addition to that, tons of old manuscripts reappeared. Forty-five years and who knows how many books later, I can't claim to know all about it—but one thing I know for sure: we won't get very far with this subject if we don't check out of Sunday school.

It looks like it's time to leave the Bible Belt and go searching elsewhere to get a deeper understanding of a process that all of us need to get a handle on—because, in case you haven't heard, Mother Earth is at the climax of a thirteen-thousand-year cycle that requires her to ascend to a new level of consciousness. Rumor has it that she's ready to make that step—and if we want to go with her, we need to find out as much as we can about the ascension process and get a clear sense of what Christ really meant when he said, *"What I do, all men can do."*

CHAPTER 2

# Connecting the Dots

Before we move on, there are a few details we need to clear up. In order to do that, it will help us to begin by backtracking to the point in the biblical description of the ascension in which the apostles ask Christ, *"Lord, is it at this time that You are restoring the kingdom to Israel?"*

For those unfamiliar with that phraseology, the restoration of the kingdom to Israel is a reference to the New Jerusalem, or the post-apocalyptic earthly paradise described by the apostle John in his Book of Revelations.

Christ's response to their question is very clear:

> It is not for you to know times or epochs which the Father has fixed by his own authority; but you shall receive power when the Holy Spirit has come upon you; and you shall be My witnesses both in Jerusalem, and in all Judea and Samaria, and even to the remotest part of the earth.[1]

He comes right out and tells them that things of this nature are none of their business and, perhaps, beyond their comprehension. Christ goes on to remind them that it's their job to open their hearts to the Holy Spirit so that they can embody it and be as living witnesses who spread his teachings *"even to the remotest part of the Earth."* The implication is that both the dissemination of his teachings and the restoration of the kingdom to Israel will take time. It is also implied that one might be contingent upon the other.

Later on in the Bible, John's revelations buttress that thought with many references to the *"last days"* or to the *"final days"* or to the *"coming of the day of the Lord"* as being the point in time when paradise will be restored. That idea is further supported in a sermon delivered by Peter on the day of the Pentecost. Drawing on the words of the prophet Joel, among other things, this dose of fire and brimstone makes it clear that it will take a while for mankind to awaken to Christ Consciousness:

"And it shall be in the last days," God says, "that I will pour forth my spirit upon all mankind; and your sons and daughters shall prophesy, and your young men shall see visions, and your old men shall dream dreams; even upon my bondslaves, both men and women, I will in those days pour forth of my spirit and they shall prophesy. And I will grant wonders in the sky above, and signs on the earth beneath, blood and fire, and vapor of smoke. The sun shall be turned into darkness, and the moon into blood, before the great and glorious day of the Lord shall come. And it shall be that everyone who calls on the name of the Lord shall be saved."[2]

We've been waiting for nearly two thousand years, wondering if and when these events would ever take place, and Peter's words have yet to be fulfilled. It would have been nice if the good book included a few dates. In reference to the coming of the day of the Lord, all we have to go on is an enigmatic statement from Peter who tells us that *"with the Lord, one day is as a thousand years, and a thousand years is as one day."*[3] How mysterious. What could this possibly mean?

What's left of the Bible raises more questions than it answers, but we can read between the lines well enough to see that there's a definite connection between the ascension, Christ Consciousness, the last days, and the restoration of the kingdom to Israel. Now that we've given ourselves permission to look elsewhere, let's call upon other sources of wisdom to see if we can frame the time that Christ spent on Earth within the context of the larger evolutionary cycles, or the "'times and epochs," that govern the planet as a whole—because what the Bible turned into an impenetrable mystery isn't that hard to figure out, once you start to look around. Contrary to what we've been led to believe, even though Christ's mission was profoundly significant, it was only part of a much bigger process that began eleven thousand years before he was born.

## The Christ Mission and Its Relationship to the Grand Cycle

The Earth is a rotating body that spins, along with the moon and the other planets in the solar system, around our sun. The sun, in its turn, spins around the galactic center in an orbit that, from an earthly perspective, appears to move in reverse at a rate of one degree every seventy-two years. If you multiply seventy-two times three-hundred-and-sixty degrees, it comes out to 25,920, or approximately twenty-six thousand years; this is about how long it takes for our sun to make one trip around the galaxy.

For one half of that cycle, the entire solar system is close enough to galactic center to be bathed in the light that streams out from the heart of creation. During the other half of the journey, we spend about thirteen thousand years circling through the darkness of what many refer to as the galactic night. This process of moving in and out of the light is formally known as the Grand Cycle and it has been going on since the beginning of time.

At the point in the Grand Cycle where we begin to shift out of the darkness, everything in creation experiences an awakening or an uplifting in consciousness. This begins well before we actually cross the divide that marks the end of the old cycle and the beginning of the new one. This awakening process is not instantaneous; it happens slowly over a long period of time, but it is always a precursor to what, from both an astrological and an astronomical perspective, is referred to as the Great Shift of the Ages.

Approximately thirteen thousand years ago, at the time of the Great Flood, or what in the esoteric and Indigenous traditions is associated with the fall of Atlantis, we entered the dark half of the Grand Cycle. From an astronomical perspective, at that time our solar system was prescessing, or moving backward, through the zodiac across the Virgo–Leo boundary. The next leg of the circuit would take us through the constellations Leo, Cancer, Gemini, Taurus, Aries, and Pisces. Spending approximately twenty-one hundred

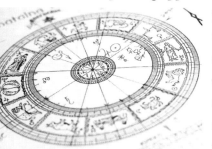

years in each sign, it would be thirteen millennia before we entered the Age of Aquarius, emerging from the darkness to begin the light half of a new twenty-six-thousand-year cycle.

The Piscean Age began right around the time Christ was born. It's no coincidence that the "Lamb of God," the one who instructed his disciples to become "fishers of men," happened to incarnate in a physical body at the point in the cosmic timeline when the Age of Aries (The Ram) gave way to the Age of Pisces (The Fish). What only becomes clear when we stop making Christ the be-all and end-all and frame his mission within the context of the evolution of the planet as a whole is that he showed up at the tail end of the Grand Cycle, armed with all kinds of important information—not to make himself the centerpiece of a new religion but to prepare humanity for a shift in consciousness that was due to coincide with our entrance into the Aquarian Age.

The following quote from the *Aquarian Gospel of Jesus the Christ* alludes to this; in a post-resurrection appearance, Jesus makes it known to the wise men of India that his triumph over death was less about him and more about what he came to encode in the collective mind:

> The magian priests were in the silence in Persepolis. . . . And Jesus came and sat with them; a crown of light was on his head. . . . And all the priests and masters stood and said, All hail! What message from the royal council do you bring? And Jesus said, my brothers of the Silent Brotherhood . . . the problem of the ages has been solved; a son of man has risen from the dead; has shown that human flesh can be transmuted into flesh divine. Before the eyes of men this flesh in which I come to you was changed with speed of light from human flesh.

And so I am the message that I bring to you. To you I come, the first of all the race to be transmuted to the image of the I AM. What I have done, all men will do; and what I am, all men will be.[4]

In this version of the tale, Christ doesn't say, "What I do all men *can* do"; his words are "What I have done all men *will* do; and what I am all men *will* be." The implication is that the work he did during his time on Earth was meant to seed something and that at some point in the future whatever he seeded would awaken all men to the Christed being within themselves. If the heart of his mission involved having to attain that level himself so that his living example would serve both as proof that it could be done and as a template for its actualization, it was because all of humanity would need to a) believe in the possibility and b) have a means to bring it about within themselves by the time we entered the Age of Light.

There's too much to suggest that the restoration of the kingdom to Israel and our entrance into the Aquarian Age are one and the same thing. What the Bible refers to as the New Jerusalem is identical to what the astrologers and the New Age aficionados tell us will usher in two thousand years of harmony and peace. And because we already know that the Great Shift is always attended with a consciousness shift, we can assume that the ascension codes are alive and just about ready to be activated inside each one of us. That process began with the Christ mission. It shifted into first gear a little over one hundred years ago, with the advent of the Theosophical movement, and went into overdrive back in 1998 when we made our formal entrance into the Age of Light.

The question is: can we take him at his word? Just because Christ told us *"what I have done, all men will do; and what I am, all men will be,"* how can we be sure? Is there any guarantee that we'll be able to light up those codes when the time comes for humanity to ascend?

## The Seeds of Christ Consciousness

In addition to providing us with a template, Christ had twelve disciples who, after his resurrection and ascension, were instructed to disseminate his message to the four corners of the Earth. Those seeds comprised the outer mysteries, or the outer teachings, of the early Christian church—but there were inner mysteries, too, and the secrets of Christ's inner circle did more to spread the word than two thousand years of preaching.

As far as the apostles go, the Bible tells us about the men, but nowhere does it mention Mary Magdalene's discipleship. Up until the mid-1940s, we were content with the idea that she was nothing but a penitent whore, but the discovery of the Nag Hammadi Scrolls changed all of that. Unearthed by an Arab peasant in 1945, thirteen papyrus documents that had been buried near the Dead Sea back in the fourth century offered clear proof that, far from being a prostitute, Mary Magdalene was Christ's number one disciple. The following quotes from Lynn Pinknett's *Mary Magdalene: Christianity's Hidden Goddess* shed light on the Magdalene's true identity:

It has always been assumed that "all the apostles" simply meant the men—what else could it mean, for surely everyone knows that Jesus only had male Apostles? While there are objections among Christians even now about allowing—often extremely reluctantly—Mary Magdalene and the other women like Joanna and Salome into the general mass of "disciples," there is strong evidence from the Gnostic texts that she was not merely a disciple, but actually the leader of the Apostles. The Gnostic "heretics" commonly referred to her as the "Apostle of the Apostles" (*Apostola Apostolorum*), or even more explicitly "The First Apostle," believing that Jesus had given her the title: indeed, according to the Nag Hammadi and other Gnostic accounts, he went even further, referring to her as "The All" and "The Woman Who Knows All," reinforcing the idea that she alone of all of his followers, male or female, knew his inner secrets. And it may not be a coincidence that the great Egyptian goddess of love, Isis, was (also) known as "The All."[5]

Ms. Pinknett's commentary on a quote from the Gospel of Thomas goes on to indicate that there was even more to the connection between the Master and the whore:

> The companion of the Savior is Mary Magdalene. But Christ loved her more than all the disciples, and used to kiss her often on her mouth. The rest of the disciples were offended. . . . They said to him, "Why do you love her more than all of us?" . . .
>
> There is distinct evidence that this was not a platonic relationship. . . . The word used for "companion" in this particular passage says it all. This is the Greek, "koinonos," which specifically means "consort" or "companion of a sexual nature," an intimate partner and—by implication—sharer in her lover's most private thoughts, not simply a close friend in God. If the disciples, both male and female, were merely fond of the first-century equivalent of New Age hugs, the acrid jealousy of the men would be hard to understand, but if the likes of Simon and Peter believed that although he should have been part of Jesus' inner circle—as indeed do all Christians everywhere—gallingly, his Master was more inclined to spend his time with this woman, all is explained. Here the disciples express their offence at the fact that

Jesus and Mary were, in the fashionable language of the day, an "item"—which they clearly felt was to their own detriment on the mission. One can almost hear them asking, "Who is this woman who knows all our Lord's secrets, and is always with him, night and day?"[6]

Many are of the mind that Mary was not only his chief disciple and lover, she was also his wife; but it's quite clear that she was no ordinary spouse. Information that has been preserved in the Templar doctrines, along with the recently revealed secrets of the Prieure of Sion, tell us that the Holy Grail of legend, rather than being the chalice that held Christ's blood after the crucifixion, was in fact, the womb of the Magdalene. The authors of *Holy Blood, Holy Grail* speak to this idea:

> The Holy Grail would have been at least two things simultaneously. On the one hand, it would have been Jesus' bloodline and descendants—the "Sang Raal," the "Real" or "Royal" blood, of which the Templars, created by the Prieure de Sion, were appointed guardians. At the same time, the Holy Grail would have been, quite literally, the receptacle or vessel that received and

contained Jesus' blood. In other words, it would have been the womb of the Magdalene—and by extension, the Magdalene herself. . . . The Holy Grail then, would have symbolized both Jesus' bloodline and the Magdalene, from whose womb that bloodline issued.[7]

Even though the defenders of the faith refuse to openly acknowledge that Christ and the Magdalene had children together, it has long been known that the two gave birth to at least one child. Jesus was no eunuch, anymore than Mary was a whore, and what needs to be understood is that their union was an alchemical fusion between a fully conscious male and a fully enlightened female.

If the act of making love served as a vehicle for their spiritual development, underneath it all, it had a deeper intent—because what Jesus and the Magdalene conceived in a state of pure consciousness, and the high-test bloodline that issued from it, was a form of High Magic that was meant to inseminate the codes for Christ Consciousness directly into the collective DNA. Both of them knew this—and what they understood equally well was that in two thousand years' time, this dissemination process would disperse those codes *even to the remotest parts of the Earth* and ultimately open the space for everyone on the planet to awaken to the Christed being within themselves.

# Are We
# There Yet?

Although astrologers differ on the exact date, by my calculations we officially entered the Aquarian Age back in 1998. The Great Shift of the Ages is upon us. The dark half of the Grand Cycle is over and the light half of the next twenty-six-thousand-year cycle is ready to begin. Those of us who pay attention to these things understand that the planet and everything on it

is about to ascend—and out of all the questions we need to be asking ourselves right now, the one that has to do with getting through the Eye of the Needle may be the only one that matters.

Christ didn't die for our sins, and he wasn't putting us on when he told us, *"What I do all men will do; and what I am all men will be."* He lived so that the ascension template, along with his outer teachings, and the genetic imprint that issued from his union with the Magdalene would be firmly rooted in the collective unconscious by the time the Grand Cycle came to an end. When Christ said, *"It shall be in the last days that I will pour forth my spirit on all mankind,"* he wasn't telling us that he would be the one to come back and redeem us—he was saying that when the time came for us to

move into the sign of the Water Bearer, the seeds that he sowed two thousand years ago would pour forth and that it would be the Christ Consciousness *in us* that would take us to the next grid level.

If all of the above isn't enough to help you understand why the ascension issue is such a big one, the Indigenous traditions tell us that we are now in the time of the Fifth Sun and are about to emerge into what they refer to as the Fifth World. Interestingly, at this point, it is the Elders of the Indigenous tribes who know more about what's happening on the planet than anyone else; and what they are telling us is that, prior to our entrance into the Fifth World, we will go through a period of devastation and purification, after which the planet will become beautiful and new again, the way it was before The Fall. According to the Indigenous Elders, as of May 2009, we were a little over a year away from the point at which the Earth will make her transition.

This is why we need a guidebook—because we're right on the verge of changes that haven't happened in such a long time, we have no memory of them and absolutely no sense of what to expect. As oxymoronic as it may seem to think about preparing for something like this, there's a lot we can do. Most of it involves accepting the fact that we're the ones that will have to live through it—the rest of it has to do with understanding that this is a frequency shift and making it through has more to do with where we are vibrationally than it does with where we're at physically; but let's not get ahead of ourselves.

The reason I took the time to frame the ascension process in both a biblical and an evolutionary context is because anything we talk about from here on out will be pointless if you don't understand that this isn't just a bunch of New Age phony baloney, and it isn't just a pile of Fundamentalist dogma; it is a very real and integral part of a major evolutionary cycle. And it's no accident that all of us chose to be here for this; somewhere inside we know that we are the ones who came to restore the Kingdom to Israel. We are also the children of the Aquarian Age and the spirits who chose to live in the time of the Fifth Sun.

By the time our bell bottoms wore out, we were already talking about these things. Since that time, so much has been written on the Great Shift and the ascension phenomena that we've got information coming out of our ears. As much as the New Age booksellers have tried to enlighten us on the subject, most of us aren't any clearer about it than we were back in the old days. Now that the reality of the actual experience is clearly imminent, let's use this field guide to strip away any confusion we have and see if we can find a way to understand what we need to do and who we need to be when it comes time for everything to shift.

## CHAPTER 3

# The "Who's Who" of Ascension

The Bible tells us that we were made in the image of Christ, and it makes it very clear that we came here to follow his example; but that's as far as it goes. Nowhere does it say that we *are* Christ or mention anything about the fact that we might be capable of exactly the same level of attainment. At some point, that information was probably included in the text, but when the Niocene Council chopped up the good book, they made sure that what we were left with would lead us to think that it would be a sin for any human being to presume that they could ever be that perfect. This may be why the thought that we could refine our sensitivities to the point we could leave this world with the physical vehicle intact, rise up to the higher levels, and even go so far as to reappear in the flesh, when and if it became necessary, is pretty hard to believe.

Christ may have been *"the first of all the race to be transmuted to the image of the I AM,"* but he was not the only one by any means; come to find out there is a long list of people who have gone through the same process—and there are probably many others who found their way to the ascension portal accidentally and never received any publicity for it. I don't know about you, but somehow or other, knowing that the most perfect person who ever lived wasn't the only one to ever have this experience, takes some of the pressure off and creates a sense of safety in numbers that makes it easier to believe that we could do it too.

# The Ascended Masters

Next to Christ, Buddha is probably the most famous ascended soul. He incarnated about four or five hundred years before Jesus was born, which means that he made his ascension long before the Magi had even spotted the Eastern Star. At the age of eighty, he announced that he was ready to leave this world and ascended bodily into heaven illuminated by an aura of bright white light. His last words were: *"All composite things pass away. Strive for your own liberation with diligence."*

We can't bring up Christ or Buddha without discussing the Ascended Masters; both of them are members of that illustrious brotherhood. The books tell us that there are seventy-two Ascended Masters and that they are otherwise known as Mahatmas, Elder Brothers, the Great White Brotherhood, and/or the Masters of Wisdom. It is believed that these beings are individuals who once incarnated here on the Earth plane and who mastered their life lessons by fulfilling their Dharma (life purpose) and burning off at least 51 percent of their negative Karma. God-like even in the flesh, after their ascension each one of them reunited with their God-Self and, like Christ, became transmuted into the image of the "I AM."

The Mahatmas live on a higher octave of the Third Dimension, and, for the most part, they oversee from the invisible realms everything that takes place here on Earth. But because they have the ability to descend into matter, during times of great change some of the Masters re-enter the physical and walk among us. Whenever the astrological ages shift, they are always there in full force, in spirit or in the flesh, to guide us through whatever those changes involve.

A little over a century ago, about a hundred years shy of the Great Shift of the Ages, some of the members of the Great White Brotherhood began to make themselves known to a small circle of spiritual seekers who were connected with the Theosophical movement and the teachings of Madame Blavatsky. Much has been written about the Elder Brothers since the dear Madame introduced them to the public. The following quote from William Q. Judge's classic *The Ocean of Theosophy* was written at the peak of the Theosophical craze, and it speaks eloquently about the role that the Masters of Wisdom play in human affairs:

The most intelligent being in the universe, man, has never, then, been without a friend, but has a line of Elder Brothers who continually watch over the progress of the less progressed, preserve the knowledge gained through aeons of trial and experience, and continually seek for opportunities of drawing the developing intelligence of the race on this and other globes to consider the great truths concerning the destiny of the soul. These Elder Brothers also keep the knowledge they have gained of the laws of nature in all departments, and are ready when cyclic law permits to use it for the benefit of mankind. They have always existed as a body, all knowing to each other, no matter in what part of the world they may be, and all working for the race in many different ways. In some periods they are well known to the people and move among ordinary men whenever the social organization, the virtue, and the development of the nations permit it. For if they were to come out openly and be heard of everywhere, they would be worshipped as gods by some and hunted as devils by others. In those periods when they do come out some of their number are rulers of men, some teachers, a few great philosophers, while others remain still unknown except to the most advanced of the body.

It would be subversive of the ends they have in view were they to make themselves public in the present civilization, which is based wholly on money, fame, glory, and personality. For this age, as one of them has already said, "is an age of transition," when every system of thought, science, religion, government, and society is changing, and men's minds are only preparing for an alteration into that state which will permit the race to advance to the point suitable for these Elder Brothers to introduce their actual presence to our sight. They may truly be called the bearers of the torch of truth across the ages; they investigate all changing things and beings; they know what man is in his innermost nature, and what his powers and destiny, his state before birth and the states into which he goes after the death of his body; they have stood by the cradle of nations and seen the vast achievements of the ancients, watched sadly the decay of those who had no power to resist the cyclic law of rise and fall.[1]

There are seventy-two Ascended Masters. At this point, all of their names have not been revealed, but here is a short list of those who are known to us: Merlin, Kwan Yin, Mary the Mother of Jesus, Enoch, Kuthumi, Abraham, Serapis Bey, Mother Teresa,

Mohammed, Krishna, Yogananda, Annalee Skarin, Hilarion, Confucius, Djwhal Khul, Master Morya, Lao-Tzu, Babaji, Pope John Paul II, and the Comte Saint Germain.

## Saint Germain

Out of all the people on that list, Saint Germain is of particular interest to us now because he is the *"Chohan of the Seventh Ray."* According to the Theosophists, the Seven Rays are seven metaphysical principles that govern both individual souls and the unfolding of each astrological age. The Seventh Ray just so happens to hold rulership over the Aquarian Age, and Saint Germain, as the *"Chohan of the Seventh Ray"* is considered to be the *"Hierarch of the Age of Aquarius."* Also known as *"The God of Freedom for the Earth,"* it could be said that he is the chairman of the committee of Masters who have been elected to superintend our passage through the Great Shift.

Born in 1710, the handsome courtier, whose occult interests and alchemical abilities reputedly gave him God-like powers, Saint Germain claimed to be hundreds of years old. The myths that surround his origins and his life have obscured the facts, but we do know that he died in 1784. A hundred years later, in the predawn of the Aquarian Age, he began to appear more and more in the physical. Since that era, reports of meetings with the Comte have been and continue to be commonplace enough to make it seem as if he has definitely been here on special assignment for a long time.

Madame Blavatsky conversed with him regularly and was quite open about the fact that Saint Germain was one of the Masters who helped her write the *Secret Doctrine*. Annie Besant, C. W. Leadbeater, Godfrey Ray King, Edgar Cayce, Paul Foster Case, and Manly P. Hall; all the great theosophists, spiritualists, and psychics claim to have met with and received instruction from Saint Germain. But it isn't just the big names that have had that privilege; ask any seeker on the New Age workshop circuit. Thousands of people have met with the Comte, and all of them are more than happy to talk about it.

Never having met him myself, I have always given the people with Saint Germain stories the benefit of the doubt. It wasn't until my friend Ron Sirchie had a real-life encounter with Saint Germain that I began to see that there might actually be some truth to all the tales. A few months after their meeting, the two of them arranged to do a videotaped interview. Having seen that footage, I have to say that I was convinced. When the time came for me to write this chapter, I decided to check in with Ron one more time just to see if he still thought that the man that he spoke with in 2008 was the real Saint Germain. What follows is a copy of the email that he sent in response to that question:

> *YES since you're asking; I just watched the video again last night. . . . YES I truly believe he was as real as it gets.*
>
> *Germain's message and the way he portrayed himself was simple and on point about staying in the heart and focusing on the positive . . . even though the negative will be there . . . focus on the positive . . . Plus his knowledge about the inner earth was awesome. . . .*
>
> *I could go on. . . . But one last thing; I remember him saying that when everything is all said and done . . . he told us that he would probably jump back in somewhere to help life rise up again. . . .*
>
> *I don't know Cal . . . I do know that he said all the correct things and I've been around, for a soon to be 40-year-old; I've hung out with Tom Kenyon, Greg Braden, Alex Grey, Ken Page (many times with Ken here on the East coast) and on and on; Saint Germain seemed true to his message. I'm actually looking to see him on the east coast again this year. I'll keep you posted.*

I realize that the idea that there are enlightened beings living on a higher level whose job it is to keep an eye on human and earthly affairs may seem totally out there to some of you—in my more logical moments, it still seems a little out there to me. At the same time, I've heard and seen enough evidence for it to be willing to loan my faith to the possibility that all of the Ascended Masters, and especially Saint Germain, are watching over us, more so now at this critical turning point, than at any other time in recorded history.

It's been said that belief is what shapes our experience. Most of us understand that what we are willing to welcome into the realm of possibility eventually comes into manifestation. If our own mastery is about to become as real for us as it is for the ones who have already made their ascension, does proof that they exist help us believe that the same level of attainment is as open to us as it was to Christ, or Buddha, or Saint Germain? Let's move on and see if a few more Ascended Master stories will answer that question for you.

## Yogananda

Yogananda is not known to be one of the guardians of the Aquarian Age, but he is significant to us and to it because he is one of the few Ascended Masters who incarnated just as the Age was dawning. Born in 1893, he began his spiritual search early in life, and at the age of seventeen, he met up with Sri Yukteswar and became his disciple. Sri Yukteswar stated that the meeting was a reunion; according to the guru, the two of them had spent many lifetimes together and that the Master Babaji had sent Yogananda to him for a very special purpose.

Well known to anyone who has an interest in spiritual development, Yogananda taught that true self-realization is the knowing in all parts of body, mind, and soul that the kingdom of God is within us. According to him, what is already ours doesn't need to be prayed for because all of us are God, and in order to experience that, all that is needed is a deep desire to cultivate and refine our relationship to that aspect of ourselves.

In the days leading up to his death, Yogananda began to hint that it was time for him to depart. On May 7, 1952, after attending a banquet, he gave a speech about world peace and ended the speech with his poem, "My India." As the last words were spoken, he collapsed on the floor, dead of a heart attack. Kriyananda, one of Yogananda's better known disciples, later said that his master had once stated in a lecture, *"A heart attack is the easiest way to die. That is how I choose to die."*

The interesting thing about Yogananda is that after his passing, his physical body never deteriorated. If you find that hard to fathom, the following quote from a notarized letter written by the director of the Forest Lawn Memorial Park Cemetery in Glendale, California, where Yogananda's body was embalmed, will make it seem more credible:

The absence of any visual signs of decay
in the dead body of Paramahansa Yogananda

offers the most extraordinary case in our experience. . . . No physical disintegration was visible in his body even twenty days after death. . . . No indication of mold was visible on his skin, and no visible drying up took place in the bodily tissues. This state of perfect preservation of a body is, so far as we know from mortuary annals, an unparalleled one. . . . No odor of decay emanated from his body at any time.[2]

Close to sixty years later, Yogananda's physical vehicle is still on ice, in pristine condition, somewhere in California. This anomaly has been the subject of much speculation. His followers are convinced that their teacher is due to return and save the world any day now. That idea may not be too farfetched; spirit goes both ways after all, and if Yogananda ascended, he is just as capable of re-entering his body when and if he chooses to.

Sri Yukteswar's awareness of Yogananda's "very special purpose" may have something to do with this. It could be that Paramahansa Yogananda's return is the miracle that will surprise us into realizing that, even for us, death is an illusion. But do we really need him to come back? Isn't the pristine condition of his body six decades after death enough to prove the point? Hello! I don't know about you, but it's enough for me; because whether Yogananda decides to reanimate his form or continues to let it rest in peace, perfectly preserved, one way or another, the lesson is the same.

# Merlin

Before we can talk about Merlin from an intelligent frame of reference, we need to get around the fairy tale and blow a little life into him; because contrary to what we've been told, the legendary Druid was real live human being. Give yourself a few minutes to clear that hurdle, because the next one involves exchanging the image of the mythical wizard with the magic wand and the pointy hat for the idea that the man we've turned into a Walt Disney character is, in fact, an Ascended Master.

If we've reduced the real Merlin to a fantasy figure, it isn't entirely our fault. Between the oral traditions of the Druids and the inventiveness of Celtic historians who, when they finally got around to writing things down, took it upon themselves to reinvent a past that they knew very little about, what's left of Merlin leaves us with nothing to go on but the King Arthur legends—and unfortunately, we are lost when it comes to them, too. Far be it from me to set the record straight, but I will try.

If you do enough research, you soon find out that the Druids were not indigenous to the British Isles. Come to find out, they originated in Atlantis and migrated to Egypt after The Fall. Their culture and their spiritual practices reemerged there, along with the Coptic and the Essene brotherhoods, approximately five hundred years before the birth of Christ. The three sects worked together to lay the spiritual foundations that would later support the Christ mission.

We know that Merlin was a Druid and that he was the leader of that sect, but few of us are aware that the name that we have come to associate with the Gandolfian character of myth isn't a name; *it is a title.* The "Merlin" is the position that is held by the leader, or the High Priest, of the Druid faith. For the followers of that faith, the "Merlin" is comparable to what the "Dalai Lama" would be for the Buddhists or what the "Pope" is to the Catholics. Passed down through lineage descent, at times when earthly affairs call for it, that position is bestowed upon an Ascended Master.

The Merlin that we are familiar with is said to have lived anywhere between 400 and 600 AD. The story goes that he was a "Halfling" with supernatural abilities, and the rest of the legend is filled with accounts that testify to his magical powers. Underneath all the fairy tales, the Ascended Master who held the position of the Merlin during the fifth century AD was indeed a magus of the highest order. His reputation for wizardry and his affiliation with Arthur and the Templar Knights (the Knights of the Round Table) are both based on fact. It is also known that the Merlin prepared Druid initiates for the ascension process at his mystery school on the Island of Avalon and at the circles at Avebury and Stonehenge. Folklore has it that the secrets of the Druidic faith are buried deep in the soil of the Glastonbury Tor.

There may be some truth to that tale because beyond his role as the Druid High Priest, this particular Ascended Master was sent to Earth for a very specific

purpose; one that involved helping humanity shift away from traditions that the Druids had upheld for a thousand years into the belief patterns that we have come to associate with Christianity. The Arthurian legends touch upon that issue, but just barely. The truth is, the man who held the position of the Merlin during King Arthur's time came here to preserve a body of wisdom that was about to go underground for fifteen hundred years. As the High Priest and guardian of those traditions, it was his job to pack them up and store them away until the time came for us to return to them.

Would it be too much to presume that in this age of transition, as humanity goes through a shift which will ultimately bring us back to the old ways, that the Merlin who was chosen to guard that wisdom is here now to assist in its restoration? The following story seems to suggest that he is.

## Drunvalo Melchizedek's Conversation with the Merlin

I don't know how many of you are familiar with Drunvalo Melchizedek, but those of you who are know that he is the disseminator of the Flower of Life Teachings. He is also someone who is deeply involved in all of the changes that are happening on the planet right now. I've been his student for about twelve years, and one of the things I enjoy most about Drunvalo is the way things happen to him; he is a magnet for some of the weirdest, wildest, most miraculous experiences I've ever heard of. His stories are incredible and all of them are true.

This story goes back to the early 1990s when Drunvalo was asked to take a trip to England to investigate the crop circle phenomenon. Because most crop circles are formed near Britain's stone megaliths, his research involved a lot of time spent at Stonehenge and some of the other stone circles for which the British Isles are so famous.

On the day that Drunvalo arrived at Stonehenge, he did what most spiritually oriented people do when they visit this sacred site: he propped himself up against a big rock and went into a meditation. After a few minutes in silence, a voice came to him and told him to leave Stonehenge and go to the stone circle at Avebury and wait.

Trusting this message, Drunvalo found his way to Avebury, sat down near the first stone he was drawn to, closed his eyes, and went into another meditation. It didn't take long for the same voice to come in; it was a deep voice with a heavy old-English accent, and it turned out to be the Merlin. His first words were: *"Thank you for joining the program."* Not knowing what this meant, as images of crop circles began to appear on the screen of his inner vision, Drunvalo listened closely while the Merlin took about forty-five minutes to explain that he and the Ascended Masters were behind the crop circle phenomenon. His next words were, *"I will prove it to you,"* at which point he instructed Drunvalo to go to Silbury Hill.

The purpose for going to Silbury Hill was not made clear, but what happened when he got there brought him into contact with a woman by the name of Barbara Davies. Barbara runs a crop circle hotline; whenever a crop circle forms, she's the one who gets the word out. In the course of conversation, Drunvalo asked her if the Vesica Pisces symbol had ever appeared in any of the British Crop circles. Barbara told him *"No"* and went on to say, *"You're staying up in Swindon; I just heard that a new crop circle formed up there last night."* To make a long story short, Drunvalo headed up to Swindon and lo and behold, there right next to the main road, was a crop circle formed in the shape of the Vesica Pisces.[3]

If all of this feels a bit too fantastic, what can I say? Drunvalo's experience is proof enough for me.

And while the tale that tells us that the Merlin is here is totally believable, whether we buy it or not, there is another aspect to the story: the crop circles themselves.

The Great Mother is etching her wisdom into fields all over the planet; anyone can see that she is not only speaking to us, she is literally rising up out of the ground, blazing with symbols that reflect the feminine face of God. As that aspect of the divine appears to be on its way up, has our logic gone too far over the top to embrace the idea that the Merlin might be here to help us remember her ways? After all, he's the one that put them to bed. Even if we choose not to believe that, we can't ignore what Mother Earth and her etchings are trying to tell us. Think about that and let's move on to lesser mortals.

## Annalee Skarin

We've talked about a few of the ascension giants, but what about the little people? Wouldn't all of this feel closer to home if we knew that some ordinary, everyday person had made it through the Eye of the Needle? This is why I love Annalee Skarin's story. She's one of us, just an average human being, and she made her ascension in 1952.

Raised in the Mormon Church, Annalee Skarin believed in her heart that immortality could be achieved through the devout application of Christian principles. Her writings were considered heretical because while she accepted the idea that virtuous souls could die and go to heaven, she regarded that pathway as the *"dreary, back door entrance"* and openly endorsed ascension as the better alternative.

If you've ever been exposed to the iron fist of Mormon fundamentalism, it should come as no surprise that the church patriarchs weren't exactly pleased with Annalee Skarin's revelations. Accused of blasphemy for daring to suggest that all of us are God, she was excommunicated by the Latter Day Saints after the publication of her first book, *"Ye Are Gods."* Unwilling to embrace her during her life, the Mormon fold deemed Annalee worthy enough to be readmitted only after she ascended.

Her ascension story is as simple and straightforward as she was. On July 16, 1952, at the home of Sally Franchow, Annalee announced that it was time for her to depart and proceeded to vanish into thin air. Conflicting accounts as to what actually took place grew out of that event, but on the day that it happened, *The Deseret News* reported, *"Many were convinced that the woman had indeed gone heavenward."*[4]

Questions as to whether or not she actually made her translation into spirit have been raised by some. Reading through the various perspectives it soon becomes clear that those who attempt to discredit her seem to choke on the fact that her truth negates theirs.

As most of us know, the outer teachings of the Christian church are founded on the belief that we're here to emulate Christ. In the same breath, we are told that the average human being is too sinful to qualify. Other sects get around this catch-22 by maintaining that the ascension was/is a total fantasy, even for Christ, and that the whole tale is just a beautiful metaphor.

If her opponents have a problem with Annalee Skarin, it is for one reason only: when the nice lady from Idaho translated into spirit, she not only made it blatantly obvious that any one of us could do the same, she became living twentieth-century proof that, even for a woman, there is a definite pathway to heaven. Would it be stretching things too far to think that Annalee Skarin might have something to do with the rise of the Female Light, and the idea that, even an average, everyday woman could be a standard bearer for it?

If it suspends belief to think that eight more books were written after her ascension, it may help you to recall that spirit goes both ways. Aside from her purpose as a scribe, Annalee's love for her husband, Reason, and her desire to assist him in reconnecting with his God-self gave her yet another excuse to move back and forth across the veil. New Age rumor suggests that Reason and Annalee Skarin are now working as a team. They have been known to appear in the same way Saint Germain, the Merlin, and others (such as Mother Mary) do, materializing at will in order to share their truth and their experience with people all over the world. Both Annalee and Reason Skarin emphasize the importance of gratitude, praise, and love as the keys to the ascension mysteries. If they are here with us, it is because they have come to assist, which gets us to the heart of the matter.

If William Q. Judge was right when he said that:

> this is an age of transition . . . men's minds are only preparing for an alteration into that state which will permit the race to advance to the point suitable for these Elder Brothers to introduce their actual presence to our sight.

as we make our entrance into the Age of Light, do these accounts of their presence help us to see that something big enough to require it is definitely on? And, do we understand that in bearing the torch of truth across the Ages that the Masters of Wisdom are also here to teach us everything we need to know about the ascension process?

If we can stretch our minds far enough to embrace all of the above, the next question is: With so little time, what would it take to close our eyes, enter our hearts, and open the conversation? The following excerpts from Li Po's *Ascended Master Dictations* seem to suggest that all we have to do is pick up the phone:

> The Masters are behind the scenes, behind the veil. We need to learn how to draw them in closer by concentrating our consciousness on them; getting to know them through study,

making contact, reaching out to them. . . . We have to take responsibility for reaching out to them in our dimension. They cannot otherwise come into, and affect, our lives unless we give them permission either by thought, calls, or actions . . . To draw them in closer we, too, must work for the Plan, for the Light. It is easy. We can begin to feel them move closer as we draw them into our consciousness, being, and world. They will eventually expand in us and take over our world at *our* request. This is how it is done if you want to make contact. There is no big secret; except this will not work for evil intent. It will only work in love. Only love can draw us up into the Ascension.[5]

On the brink of a dimensional shift, it makes sense that all our support and instruction would come from another level. What also makes sense is the idea that only those who have been through the ascension process would be qualified to instruct us in its mysteries. If ringing up the Great White Brotherhood is too much to wrap you your mind around, ask yourself where else are you going to find the information you need right now? We can only be taught by those who have gone before us. Those who have gone before us may be invisible to our sight, but they are very much here, and my sense is that our individual and collective ascension process begins when we open our minds to include that possibility.

CHAPTER 4

# Trust Your Mother

We've looked at the ascension from a spiritual point of view, and we've learned a little bit about the *why* of it; now we need to see what it looks like from the Third Dimension and learn more about the physical changes that are all part of the process. Hold on to your hats. It's time to leave the realm of the Ascended Masters and descend into matter for a brief reality check.

## Truth and Lies

In case you haven't noticed, Hollywood has fallen madly in love with Doomsday. Grab the clicker and see for yourself; the Grand Cycle, the Great Shift, the End of Time, the secrets of the ages, and the 2012 prophesies are now the hottest item on national television. And in November 2009, a blockbuster movie took our fascination with the end of the world right over the top.

What seems to have come out of nowhere began to leak into the mainstream at least fifty years ago. Anyone who remembers will tell you that it was in the sixties that our passion for all things occult took over the collective mind. By 1970, between the old theosophical books and the New Age paperbacks, everything we never knew turned us on to things that lit up a desire for more. Since that era, our curiosity about the times we're in has gathered enough momentum for the law of supply and demand to bring the Great Shift, and everything that goes with it, from the occult bookstore all the way to the silver screen.

Between the barrage of information and our over-exposure to it, most of us have heard or read enough about the End Times to assume that we're well informed. The problem is, we are reading and watching material that, with all of the best (and sometimes the worst) intentions, is often misconceived. If some of the more recent books make an effort to get to the heart of the matter, few of them go all the way, and none of them have anything to say about what actually takes place when the Shift occurs. As far as Hollywood goes, do we even need to talk about it? They may be milking this trend for whatever it's worth, but let's not kid ourselves; the last time I tuned in to an Apocalypse special, the truth was nowhere in sight.

When something this big is no longer a subject for debate, it would seem to give us the impetus to fill ourselves in on the details. I find it amazing that it's taken this long for us to wonder what they might entail. And while we need to have a clear understanding that our passage through the Shift depends more on where we are in our hearts than anything else, there are physical and mechanical aspects to this change that, like everything in nature, follow a specific pattern.

When you think about the entire planet shifting into the next dimension, even if you understand the *why* of it, don't you wonder how the ascension process gets translated at the physical level? What actually happens when she decides to take that leap? If there are answers, it would be great to know what they are because this is the last train out of here, and I am sure that the films that sell us annihilation and the books that see it with rose-colored glasses don't tell it like it is. Those of you who wish someone would talk about it in real terms are probably still waiting for answers to the following questions:

- Are there signs that tell us that it's time?
- Do we all go at once? If not, who gets to go?
- How long does the process take?
- Is there a pattern to it?
- How will we know what to do?
- What happens when we come out on the other side?
- Will the Earth still be here?
- What will the world look like?
- What about our loved ones?
- What do we do once we get there?

These are just a few of the questions that come up for me. If there are more, they will surface as we go along. Let's see if we can dig up some answers, or at least a few clues, in the hopes that whatever we discover will lead us to a more enlightened point of view.

## Initial Signs

Every time the Earth moves from one grid level to the next, her physical body goes through a pole shift.

Before she makes that physical shift, she first has to do it inwardly by repositioning her Kundalini (the spiritual aspect of her polar axis) and attuning herself spiritually to the energies of the next evolutionary cycle. This is how she prepares herself. Whenever her Kundalini moves from one location to another, it is a sign that the Great Mother is getting ready for a pole shift. Both the energetic and the physical aspects of the shift are part of a natural process that recurs approximately every thirteen thousand years.

Up until 2008, the Kundalini of the planet was rooted in the highest mountains of Tibet. The Indigenous people of the world have always known this—and what their Wisdom Keepers have also known is that the time would soon come for what is otherwise known as the *"Serpent of Light"* to move to its new home in the mountains of Chile. That change has already occurred, and the Elders are telling us it won't be long before the Earth's poles shift in order to align themselves with the changes that took place in the subtle energy realms more than two years ago.

Science is now in agreement with the Indigenous wise men. Keeping a close eye on the Earth's magnetic field, their instruments are telling them that in certain parts of the world the force of gravity is fast approaching Zero Point. For them, this is cause for concern because the collapse of the magnetic field is the trigger mechanism that sets off a pole shift. With astrological evidence to confirm both the Indigenous and scientific perspectives, it is clear that we haven't got much time. As of April 2009, all of the Indigenous Elders concurred that the shift would occur sometime near the summer of 2010.

Unfortunately, at a time when a little truth would go a long way, the media isn't telling it. Our perceptions of what happens during a pole shift have been so heavily influenced by the disaster imagery that we see on TV and in films, we only see that side of it. And while there's no way to sidestep the cataclysmic element, if that's all we get to focus on, the fact that we're ascending and the beauty of being welcomed into that process will be overridden by the fear of annihilation. We can't allow ignorance to keep us from making the most of this experience; so let's turn off the TV and see what a pole shift looks like from Mother Earth's perspective.

# Pole Shifts Unplugged

If you look at how she's constructed, relative to her seven-thousand-mile diameter, the outer shell of the Earth is only about a hundred miles thick. Underneath her surface shell, and attached to it like the membrane that clings to the inner surface of an eggshell, is a sub-layer of granite that goes all around the world. Beneath this granite, semi-molten rock surrounds an iron core.

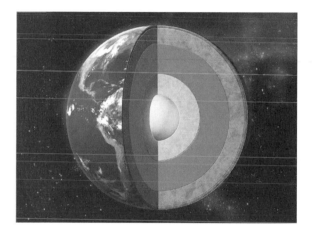

Rotating on its axis at a rate of sixty-seven thousand miles per hour, the geographical points that define that axis are the Earth's physical poles. The combined spin of the planet and the magnetism of the iron in her core produce a magnetic field that extends out beyond her body, way out into space, in the same way that the human aura surrounds the human body. This huge, toroidal energy field is the Earth's magnetic field. It has its own axis, and the poles of that axis are known as the Earth's magnetic poles.

Whenever there is a pole shift, the Earth's magnetic poles shift first. It's as if she has to make an energetic adjustment before she can adjust at the physical level. This is always the way it goes. But before the magnetic poles can shift, the magnetic field of the Earth has to go all the way down to Zero Point, or zero magnetics. The moment that happens, something amazing takes place inside Mother Earth.

As soon as the magnetic field shuts off, the magnetic poles disappear. Cut loose, with nothing to hold them in place, they begin to wander erratically in search of their new home. During this phase many things occur, but the change in magnetics serves to alter the composition of the thick granite sub-layer that we spoke of earlier, causing it to melt into a semi-liquid or oily state. With nothing to keep it from moving, the Earth's outer shell is now free to float over what was once solid rock.

Once the magnetic poles find their new orientation, they settle down. At that point, the physical poles shift and realign themselves with the magnetic poles. This process kicks off when the Earth's outer shell begins to slide over the liquid sub-layer. The mechanism that actually causes the outer shell to move to its new location is provided by the miles and miles of ice that have piled up unevenly at the South Pole. Off-kilter and still rotating at the same speed, as the Earth adjusts to its new spin axis the weight of the south polar ice creates an imbalance that serves to push the loose outer shell, and the Earth's physical poles, into their new position.

The earth changes that we have come to associate with our worst fears begin in earnest as soon as the magnetic field collapses; when the physical poles shift, that activity increases. Between the time the magnetic field shuts down and the point where the outer shell begins to move is when we make our ascension; when the outer shell starts to shift, for the Earth, that is the physical manifestation of what has already occurred inside both her and us. The actual physical shifting of the poles is the fait accompli that aligns the axis of the world with its new star.

My trust in the Great Mother has always been unshakable. Ever since I found out that, among all of the other incredible things she is capable of, she is also custom made for pole shifts, my faith in her has gone beyond mere reverence. Who knew that the Goddess was an expert at moving from one world to another? It boggles my mind to think that when her magnetics disappear and polarity vanishes, she knows exactly how much of herself to dissolve so that she can step out of the way and allow creation to reinvent itself. If we think Mother Earth doesn't have everything under control, we might ask ourselves why it never occurred to us that the archetypal female might be an old hand when it comes to giving birth.

When all of the above was explained to me, the "dark cloud of unknowing" that has always surrounded my End Times questions began to melt. Understanding the physics of a pole shift helped me to see that for the Earth, this really is a natural process, one that she is fully equipped for and, like any mother, probably looking forward to. And because we are her microcosmic image, the Hermetic Axiom that tells us everything is a reflection of the greater whole reminds me that the same mechanism that lives in her is alive in us; the part of us that remembers ascension will awaken the moment the Shift begins—and we don't need to worry, because like Mother Earth, each one of us has done this many times before.

We've got more questions to answer, but we can't do it all at once. This is a lot to take in, so take a deep breath and get ready to carry it one step further—because it's time to look at what happens to us while the Great Mother is on the delivery table.

CHAPTER 5

# The Road Home

Every spiritual tradition comes with its own End Times legend. The stories are all different, but what they share in common is the idea that life on this Earth is renewed in cycles and that the renewal process is always attended by a cataclysm. Back when this chapter was just a thought, I figured I could dip into the Hindu texts or the Norse myths or any of the other End Times accounts and cull enough information from all of them to speak about the "road home" from a clear and intelligent point of view. Little did I know that this plan would get me nowhere.

Unfortunately, when it comes to hard facts that relate to the actual physics of human ascension, none of the sacred books tell it like it is. No matter which source you go to, even if you're a whiz at reading between the lines, there are no tips on how we're supposed to conduct ourselves, no details that describe what we'll meet along the path, nor anything that frames the process in a context that allows there to be both a point and a pattern to the experience.

As much as I love looking at life from every possible angle, at the moment I am less concerned with giving the various End Times legends the respect they deserve than I am with giving you something to go on. Time is too short for us to be deciphering symbols and poring over metaphors that don't come with any practical advice. Aside from that, the story is always the same; and while every culture has its own way of telling it, the plot inevitably sounds a lot like the following passage from the gospel of Luke:

> There will be signs in the sun and the moon and the stars; on Earth nations in agony, bewildered by the clamor of the ocean and its waves; men dying of fear as they await what menaces the world, for the powers of heaven will be shaken. And then they will see the Son of Man coming in a cloud with power and great glory. When these things begin to take place, stand erect, hold your head up high, because your liberation is near at hand.[1]

I encourage those of you who are truly interested in these things to look around and see what the different prophets and spiritual traditions have to say about the End of Time—but since we happen to be *in* it, for the purposes of this discussion I think it would be more helpful to focus on sources of wisdom that can actually tell us how it goes and what to expect along the way.

Out of all the information I have come across, the only ones who seem to have any hard facts about the End Times mysteries are the Indigenous peoples. There is a reason for this. They are the keepers of the teachings that were passed down by the Creator at the beginning of this time cycle. The only members of the human tribe who have maintained their connection to

Mother Earth, generations of Indigenous Elders have kept an eye on her patterns for thirteen thousand years.

It was their ancestors who lived through the last dimensional shift—and the records of what took place at the time of the Atlantis cataclysm were preserved in oral traditions that have been passed down through lineage descent to the present-day wisdom keepers. Deeply attuned to her cycles, the Indigenous peoples not only know what is coming, they know more about how it goes than anyone on the planet.

Closely guarded by a network of Elders, those secrets have been inaccessible to us until recently. It's hard to say exactly when they started coming out, but in 2008, the Elders from all of the Indigenous tribes made it known that they were concerned about the pole shift and that its imminence was prompting them to share with the rest of the world certain things that are known only to them.

Aside from the Indigenous Wisdom Keepers, Drunvalo Melchizedek is the only other source who talks about the End Times in a down-to-earth way. He has spoken openly and in detail about them for quite some time. Since the mid-1980s, Drunvalo has traveled and taught all over the world, sharing a body of information that focuses directly on the human and planetary ascension process and the need to prepare ourselves for it.

He is also deeply connected to the ways of the Native American people. With full recall of his only other Earthly experience as a Kachina medicine woman of the Taos Tribe, his current life purpose is directly related to things that his spirit set in motion back in the 1840s. This would all seem to be open to question were it not for the fact that *all* of the Indigenous Elders recognize Drunvalo and consider him to be one of them.

At this point, time and circumstance have made him their liaison with the outside world—and because Drunvalo seems to be a conduit for all of the information that is pouring out of the Indigenous sector, his writings and video presentations go into the nuts-and-bolts aspects of the ascension process in more detail than anything I have come across in forty years—and everything he has to say coincides with the way the Elders tell it.

I see no point in beating around the bush; time is too short for us to be wondering what Luke really meant when said our *"liberation is near at hand."* If the Indigenous wisdom and Drunvalo's work are the only sources that offer any practical advice, let's look at that information and see if it helps clarify things that will only be frightening to us if we remain satisfied with generalizations that speak to us metaphorically.

Before we start, you need to know that what you're about to read will sound like something out of a science fiction movie to many of you. If it stretches the limits of belief, ask yourself this question: *what makes you think a dimensional shift would operate within the boundaries of Earthly logic?* Loosen up. Expand your mind and your pictures to include just about anything—because as we all know, the truth is stranger than fiction.

## The Preliminary Breakdown Phase

Indigenous wisdom tells us that the first signs of a pole shift show up when the structures that support the existing civilization begin to break down. When the outer political, religious, educational, economic, and ecological systems start to disintegrate, in essence the pole shift has already begun.

Examining our current situation, it doesn't take much to see that this part of the process is well underway. It began at the energetic level in October 2007, when the harbinger of the End Times, the Blue Star of Hopi prophecy, appeared in the heavens. To the scientific community it became known as Comet Holmes, but to the Elders it was much more than just a comet. Blue in color, it came out of nowhere to fulfill an ancient prophecy that states: "*When the Blue Star makes its appearance in the heavens the Fifth World will emerge.*" Signs and portents notwithstanding, this one packed a wallop; within a year, the financial systems of the world collapsed, forcing us to recognize that, for a civilization that has come to value money over all other things, it wouldn't take long for the domino effect to bring everything down.

According to the Elders, this preliminary breakdown phase lasts no more than two years and no less than three months. Calculating from October 2007, the three-month window closed in January 2008; by October 2009 the two-year timeframe expired. This book was completed prior to that date, but if their wisdom is correct, I am sure that the news reports that came out at the end of October 2009 showed that outer chaos was on the rise. Hard astrological aspects between Pluto, Saturn, and Uranus that were due to converge at that point suggest that this would have been the case; and if the fluctuations in the Earth's magnetic field were causing jumbo jets to vanish into thin air as early as May 2009, we can safely assume that those influences were even more active when the initial breakdown phase ended.

We don't need to look at the calendar; all we need to do is look around. The signs are everywhere. If we aren't already thinking in terms of a pole shift, we need to start thinking about it and begin to prepare ourselves in earnest. Since we're here to find out as much as we can about what that might entail, let's see what the Indigenous traditions tell us about the early warning signs and the Three Days of Darkness that are due to coincide with our entrance into the Fifth World.

## Five or Six Hours Before

From what I have heard and read, the signs that tell us that the poles are about to shift become more than apparent approximately five or six hours before the magnetic field finally goes down. The way I understand it, as elements of the new reality begin to filter into the old one, we see Fourth Dimensional objects floating around here in 3D, shapes and forms that are unlike anything we have ever seen before. The following quote from the second volume of *The Ancient Secret of the Flower of Life* explains this in more detail:

> This phase is a weird one, from a human point of view. The Native Americans in the tribe I was first born to when I arrived on Earth, the Taos Pueblo, are told to enter the pueblo, pull the curtains, not look outside, and pray. To look outside would only cause fear, which is the last thing you need.

A strange phenomenon begins at this stage. The two dimensions begin to overlap. You may be sitting in your room when suddenly something appears out of nowhere that will not be explainable to your mind. It will be a Fourth Dimensional object that does not fit into your understanding of reality. You will see colors that you have never seen before in your life. These colors will be exceedingly bright, and they'll seem to have their own light source. The color will seem to be emitted rather than reflected. And they have a shape your mind will not be able to explain. These objects will be the strangest things you have ever seen. It is okay; it is a natural phenomenon.

My strong suggestion to you is, *don't touch* one of these objects. If you do, it will instantly pull you into the Fourth Dimension at an accelerated rate. It would be easiest and best if you avoid moving that fast. If it is unavoidable, then it is the will of God.[2]

When these Fourth Dimensional objects begin to appear, things start to feel a little strange to us. There's a sense of lightheadedness and disorientation that derives from the magnetic changes that have begun and are about to intensify. As the magnetic field goes all the way down to Zero Point, all of our artificial systems, structures, and devices, along with the thought forms that hold them in place, go through an erasure process that is similar to what happens when you erase the magnetics on a tape or a CD. The change in magnetics clears the track, opening the space for something new to etch itself into the records.

The Earth changes that we have come to associate with our worst fears become active at this time; as the existing matrix disappears, Mother Earth responds with a lot of volcanic activity. The molten iron in her core and the iron filings in her lava flows are magnetic in nature. When the magnetic field collapses, those forces begin to erupt all over the planet. Cut loose from the girdle of polarity, the four elements get stirred up on every level—high winds, tidal waves, earthquakes, fires, electrical anomalies—all hell appears to break loose in this preliminary phase.

The reason the Taos Elders instruct their people to go inside, close their curtains, and pray is because so much of what we call reality disintegrates during this six-hour window, it is difficult to get through the experience if our attention and our senses are focused on the outside world. Wherever we are when these changes begin, fear and panic can only be stilled by going within. Do whatever it takes to get centered and calm. If you understand the instructions for the Mer-Ka-Ba Meditation,[3] now would be a good time to activate your Mer-Ka-Ba.

In terms of physical safety, the best place to be during this part of the process is out in nature or inside a dwelling that is made of 100 percent natural materials. Aluminum siding, foam insulation, the wiring that runs the circuits in our homes, plastic materials of any kind, and even glass and stainless steel—things that are synthetic in nature won't make it through a dimensional shift. Ironically, at this stage of the game, a grass shack would be safer than a mansion on the hill; and unless you prefer to take this ride in your birthday suit, make sure you're wearing cotton, silk, or wool.

Within five or six hours, the world as we know it will end and the Earth will enter the next phase of the ascension process. What amounts to approximately three days of Earth time is how long it will take for us to transition from one world to another. Prior to that stage of the shift, according to Drunvalo, the only thing to do is

> . . . become centered and wait, because what's about to happen is God's grace. There

really is nowhere to go. It's the greatest ride you can imagine. It is ancient yet it is brand new. It is beautiful and you feel fantastic. You feel more alive than you did when you were in the normal Earth reality. Each breath seems to be exciting.[4]

The same quote goes on to describe what we will see and sense immediately before we make our ascension:

A red, glowing fog begins to slide into the space all around you. Soon you are surrounded by this red fog, which seems to have its own source of light. It's a fog but it doesn't actually look like any fog you have ever seen before. It seems to be everywhere now. You are even breathing it.

An odd feeling comes over your body. It isn't really bad, just unusual. You notice that the red fog is slowly changing to orange. You no sooner see it is orange than it turns yellow. The yellow quickly changes to green, then blue, then violet, then ultraviolet. Then a powerful flash of pure white light explodes into your consciousness. You are not only surrounded by this white light, but it seems that you are this light. For you there is nothing else in existence.

This last feeling seems to continue for a long time. Slowly, very slowly, the white light changes into clear light and the place where you are sitting becomes visible again. Only it looks like everything is metallic and made of pure gold—the trees, the clouds, the animals, the houses, other people—except your body, which may or may not appear like pure gold.

Almost imperceptibly, the gold, metallic reality becomes transparent. Slowly everything begins to look like golden glass. You'll be able to see right through walls; you can even see people walking behind them.[5]

As the gold metallic reality begins to fade away, the light disappears and everything turns black. You will see nothing, not even your hand in front of your face. In this darkness you will be stable, but it will feel as if you are floating. With nothing remaining from the old world, and no sound or light to inform your senses, these are the signs that herald your entrance into the Great Void, or the empty space, that separates the Fourth from the Fifth World.

## Three Days of Darkness

There is nothing to be afraid of when this phase of the pole shift begins. It's best to relax and imagine yourself in the ultimate sensory deprivation chamber. It also helps to remember that, for the Earth, this is the point where her magnetic poles start to wander; it is also the point when her thick granite sub-layer dissolves.

Taking our cue from the Great Mother, as soon as the blackness envelopes us, it's best to dissolve into the experience and flow with it. Stay centered in your heart and breathe, knowing that you have just entered the Great Void, or the womb of creation, and must now allow the oneness that connects you to everything to include you in the birth process. For the next three days there is nothing to do but wait and remain in attunement with the God within. You will probably dream at this time. Enjoy your dreams. Allow them to be. They are part of the experience.

> To be concise, this period may last from two and a quarter days (the shortest ever known) to about four days (the longest ever experienced). Normally it is between three and three and a half days. These days are Earth days, of course, and the time is experiential, not real, because time as we know it does not exist. You have now reached the "end of time" that the Maya and other religions and spiritual people have spoken of.[6]

After what seems like an eternity, Drunvalo tells us:

> The next experience is rather shocking. After floating in nothing and blackness for

three days or so, on one level of your being it may seem like a thousand years have gone by. Then totally unexpected and in an instant, your entire world will explode with a brilliant white light. It will be blinding. It will be the brightest light you have ever known, and it will take a long time before your eyes can adjust and handle the intensity of this new light.[7]

In the same way that we left the darkness of the womb to be born into the Third Dimension, we emerge from the blackness of the Great Void to find ourselves on an entirely different level of consciousness. The instant the light is restored, it means that the Earth has formally shifted into the light half of the Grand Cycle, signaling our return to a state of oneness and unity that we have not experienced in more than thirteen thousand years. Blinded by the brilliance of this new reality, there will be colors and sounds and objects that will be unlike anything we have ever seen before.

Welcome to the Fifth World! Indigenous wisdom tells us that it is one of the most beautiful worlds in creation. Other spiritual traditions describe it the same way, so call it the New Jerusalem if that feels better to you. Call it Paradise, Heaven, Arcadia, Nirvana, the Age of Light, the Elysian Fields, the Kingdom of Israel—call it whatever you want; when the light returns, we will awaken in a new form on a higher octave of experience.

# Who Knew?

How does it feel, now that you know a little bit more about how it goes? It's much easier to embrace the prospect of a pole shift when you understand that what we have turned into our worst nightmare is, in fact, what all of us have been waiting for. As it turns out, we are being reborn; and like any other birth, the pangs that are about to open the womb of the Great Mother are just a precursor to the awakening of new life.

If the ascension process and the shift in consciousness that are already underway lie at the root of all the rumbling and shaking, it does more good to center ourselves and focus on that than it does to get swallowed by any fears we might have about the labor process. This isn't the end of all things; it's a whole new beginning. Now that we know a little bit about how it goes, all we have to do is pay attention, surrender to the experience, and let the signs show us the way home.

Those of you who are sure that you're going to be one of the ones who don't make it through need to remember this: the Christ Codes that Christ and Mary Magdalene seeded into the collective bloodstream two thousand years ago are alive inside each one of us. The atom of our consciousness that remembers unity is ready to wake up. When the magnetics that govern duality disappear, can we presume that that aspect of our spirit will come to life as soon as the ascension process begins? I am pretty sure that when Christ told us it would be in the Last Days that he would pour forth his spirit upon all mankind that this is what he was talking about.

Now that we're all safe at home, it would be nice to know something about what happens once we get there; and there is more to say about many of the things that we've covered here—so let's take heart from the following words and move on to look at what it's like to wake up in another dimension.

As we enter this new millennium, the ascended masters feel that there will be very little violence approaching this shift, for we have come a long way on the path. We have done a great job in helping to birth the new human consciousness! So I am going to say it now—relax, don't worry. Enjoy this transition. As you witness the perfection of life . . . Know that you are going to be taken care of and that pure love is guiding these events. This energy wave is so much bigger than you that you might as well surrender to life and just be. . . . More than likely you will wake up one morning, and before sunset find yourself a baby in a brand-new world.[8]

## CHAPTER 6

# The New Reality

Whenever the ascension question is raised, before we even stop to consider what the process involves, our first thought is always, *"where are we going, and what will it look like when we get there?"* Talking about this is tricky because it brings up the whole subject of "heaven," and everything we have come to associate with it. When was the last time you heard anyone talking about heaven as if it were a real place? Even the preachers don't go there—only intoxicated, homeless prophets rant openly about the heavenly realms—so how do we approach the subject without seeming to be as delusional as the bum with the DTs?

Before we can begin to explore the new reality, we have to get over the idea that it's either sacrilegious or totally insane to talk about heaven. Once we clear that hurdle, we have to be open to the thought that life exists in many different forms and on many different levels of experience. If we get that far, it becomes easier to embrace the possibility that what we call God, or the state of oneness that pervades everything in creation, is accessible from every dimension, but the way to it varies, depending on which realm we happen to occupy.

Here in the Third Dimension, the life force expresses the *"oneness of all that is"* in a polarized fashion. When we are connected to it, that force uses positive and negative, male and female, up and down, hot and cold, light and dark to inform us that extremes that appear to be separate and different aren't that way at all.

For example, light and dark occupy opposite poles of the light spectrum. Darkness manifests as an absence of light, but it's still light. The same holds true for hot and cold or any other pair of opposites. If the war between the sexes makes it hard to see that there's any common ground between the male and the female, lest we forget, the union of the two leads to the creation of new life. From an electromagnetic perspective, positive and negative come together and neutralize each other at the Bloch Wall, that magical place where south becomes north and north becomes south. If the illusion of duality obscures the fact that we are swimming in an ocean of oneness, it's because it takes two to tango in this dimension, and it is only through the reconciliation of opposites that we get to experience unity.

Our experience of oneness may be distorted by polarity, but at least we have a vague sense of it. The idea that there is a place where *everything is as it should be*," where life is harmonious and nothing is separate, lives inside all of us. No matter what the mind does to convince us that it's sheer lunacy to entertain notions of heaven, every now and then we have an experience that takes us there; for a split second, we light up like a firefly, illuminated by the ineffable. The minute the light goes off, we slip back into duality. Even though the laws that bind us to the Third Dimension don't allow us to live in that place on a permanent basis, glimpses of it and the realness of each experience create an indelible impression that stays with us, even when we're in the dark.

These intermittent brushes with unity have formed the basis for both our private and collective visions of paradise. Moments of consciousness, pieced together, lead us to conclude that there is another world. If we don't succumb to external pressure to discount our experience, and if life is kind enough to allow us to touch down in that place and light up from time to time, we come to understand that this other reality is as real as the one we occupy. After a while, time and repeated experience prove this beyond a shadow of a doubt.

That being said, don't you think it's high time we made it okay to talk about heaven? We've all been there, so it seems ridiculous not to. Those of you who don't buy that idea need to be reminded that it's where you came from. If you have no memory of this, it's only because those memories vanish as soon as we are born; the truth is, everyone enters the Earth plane from a higher dimension. So let's lift the ban that precludes any discussion of paradise, heaven, the land of our dreams, the next dimension—whatever you choose to call it—and give ourselves permission to be crazy enough to talk about things that are totally out of this world.

## After the Light Returns

Scrolling back to where we left off, by the time the light returns, the poles will have shifted and that aspect of the ascension process will be over. Coming out of the Great Void, after three days of absolute darkness, we will find ourselves looking out upon a whole new world with no clear sense of its laws and nothing but what happens from moment to moment to show us what they might be. Many things come into play once the physical changes that attend the ascension process are complete, and all of them have to do with getting used to the way creation expresses itself in the Fourth Dimension.

If we enter the Earth plane as tiny little beings, we ascend into the Fifth World as full-grown adults. Because the template for an adult body is a little different in the next dimension, as soon as we are born into that world, we begin to grow according to the laws that are operative on that level. The following passage from *The Ancient Secret of the Flower of Life: Volume II* begins by telling us that males grow to heights of fourteen to sixteen feet, and females grow to be ten or twelve feet tall. It goes on to explain:

> Your body will seem solid, just as on Earth, but compared to Third Dimensional Earth, it isn't. In fact, if you were to go back to Earth no one would see you. You still have an atomic structure, but the atoms will have mostly converted to energy. You have become a great deal of energy and very little matter. You can walk right through a solid wall on Earth, but

here you are solid. This new birth will be your last life in structure as you know it. In the Fifth Dimension, which will come after the Fourth, there are no life forms. It is a formless state of consciousness. You will have no body but will be everywhere at once.

Time is extremely different in the Fourth Dimension. A few minutes on Earth is several hours in 4D, so in what seems like about two years, you will reach adulthood. But simply growing up is not what life is all about, just as here on Earth. There are levels if knowledge and existence that would be hard to imagine from where you will be when you first enter the Fourth Dimension, just as a baby here on Earth could not comprehend astrophysics.[1]

The moment we arrive, who we are comes under the influence of higher light frequencies that alter us structurally and refine the physical vehicle internally. If we understand that everything about us is connected, and our consciousness is beaming up to a higher, lighter level, it makes sense that every atom in our bodies would undergo a similar transformation. The idea that we will grow to be ten to sixteen feet tall sounds unbelievable, until we realize that this might have something to do with the fact that our expanded consciousness will require a bigger and lighter container. Other sources bear this out. The following quote from a Metatron[2] channeling seems to coincide with the way Drunvalo sees it and goes into a little more detail:

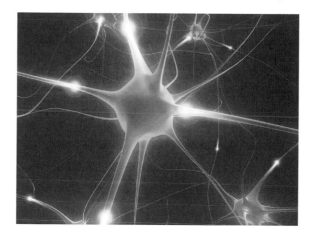

Yes, I am saying that the physical form will make its way back to the Ultimate Creator, but it will be very different from your physical body (as it is in 3D). It will not be dense but rather, the electrons of the physical will be of a different formation and there will be larger spaces between the electrons. . . . So what I mean is that the physical body will be more electrical, rather than a hard substance. . . . The physical body, from at least an external point of view will not go through many changes, but internally, there will be many changes. Internally, all the cells must be changed from an organic structure to a crystalline structure. Another way of saying this is that the cells hold light in a manner that hasn't been experienced since

Atlantis. The electrical wiring in the physical body must change also, so that the organs and the brain will accept more of the light that exists in the higher vibrational pools.[3]

It looks like this is all about fine-tuning the physical vehicle, replacing the old hard drive and upgrading obsolete patterns and programs with a system that will allow us to function on a completely different level of experience. These physical adjustments will be attended with as many mental adjustments.

Those of us who understand the power of thought and who are already aware that the outer world is a projected image of whatever we hold in our minds, know that everything we think about eventually becomes real for us. If this is hard for us to see, it's because here on Earth, the Law of Time creates a gap between the thought and the time it takes for it to manifest at the physical level. In the Third Dimension, it can take years for our dreams to become real. In the Fourth Dimension, one of the first things we'll notice is that thought and manifestation function simultaneously; the moment we think of something, it will be right there in front of us. The following quote from Drunvalo tells us how this works:

Here you are, a baby in a new world. Yet in this new world you are far from helpless. You are a powerful spirit that can control the entire reality with your thoughts. Whatever you think happens instantly! Yet at first, you normally don't recognize this connection. Most people don't put the two together for several days, and those few days are crucial. They *could* keep you from surviving in this new world if you don't understand.

Here you are, only a few minutes old, and the first big test in life begins. When the Fourth Dimensional window is opened, anyone can go through, but not everyone can stay.

What we have found is that there are three types of people at this stage. First there are the people who pass over who are ready. They have prepared themselves in this life by the way they have lived. Then there are the people who aren't ready, who are filled with so much fear that they cannot allow themselves to leave this Third Dimension past the Void, and they immediately return to Earth. Finally, there's a third group that passes over but isn't really quite ready for this experience. . . .

When people are not quite ready it means that they are bringing all their fears and hatred with them. When they find themselves in this very bizarre world, all their fears and anger arise. Because they don't know that whatever they think will take shape around them, their fears begin to manifest.

Because they don't understand what is happening, in the beginning most people reproduce familiar images of their old world, things they can recognize. They do this to make sense of what is happening. They are not doing this consciously, but from their survival instinct. They start creating the old images and emotional patterns. But this new world is so bizarre all their fears come up. They say, "Holy cow, what's going on? This is crazy, insane!" They see people who had died long ago. They might begin to see scenes from their past, even their childhood. Nothing makes sense. The mind searches for some way to create order.

They think they're hallucinating, and this brings up more fear. Thinking in their Earthly way, they might feel that someone is doing this to them, so they need to protect themselves. The ego thinks it needs a gun. Manifestation follows thought, and when they look down, there's a rifle with a scope, just what they wanted. They pick up the gun and think, "I need ammunition." They look to their left and there are huge boxes of it. They load up and begin looking for bad guys who they think are trying to kill them. So who instantly appears? The bad guys, fully armed.

Now their worst fears start manifesting, whatever they are, so they start shooting.

Everywhere they turn, other people are trying to kill them. Finally their biggest fear manifests, and they are fatally shot.

A scenario of some sort will happen that will remove them from this higher world back to the world from which they came. This is what Jesus meant when he said, "For all they that take the sword shall perish with the sword." But Jesus also said, "Blessed are the meek, for they shall inherit the Earth," which means that if you're sitting in this new world thinking simple thoughts of love, harmony, and peace, trusting in God and yourself, then that is exactly what you will manifest in your world. You will manifest a harmonious, beautiful world. If you are "meek," you allow yourself to remain in this higher world by your thoughts, feelings, and actions. You survive.[4]

Part of the reason the power of thought, positive affirmations, and all the self-help systems that tell us we create our own reality have become so popular in the last four or five decades is because those things are all part of the wake-up call that has been going on behind the scenes for more than a hundred years. What we call New Age thought, isn't new; it's old information, information that has been hidden for thirteen thousand years—but because we are being prepared to cross over into a realm where those concepts are fundamental to our survival, the spiritual systems and the self-help methods that have mushroomed since the 1960s and '70s have served to give us a heads-up on knowledge that will be indispensable to us during the ascension process and even more valuable as we begin to find our way in the new reality.

## Living in the Now

The first thing we learn when we embark on the spiritual path is the importance of living in the moment. Baba Ram Dass brought this to our attention forty years ago, and Eckhart Tolle is still talking about it today. No matter who you read or which seminar you go to, the bottom line in every New Age thought system revolves around staying in present time.

Beyond the fact that it makes it much easier to enter a meditative state, cultivating the ability to "be here now" is the only way that we in the Third Dimension can get out of our minds and experience the sense of timelessness that exists on the next level. If knowing this has improved our inner work, from an evolutionary perspective, it was meant to prepare the collective mind to shift into Unity Consciousness. Dr. Robert Pettit, author of *You Can Avoid Physical Death: Physical Body Ascension to the New Earth* elaborates on the connection between the "Now" moment and the evolution of consciousness:

Ascending humans are to become masters of time. We all realize that our human spirits chose to go through "The Fall" and live within the world of illusory time and space on the Third Dimension Earth. However, we are not bound by the illusion of time and space from a spiritual perspective. We are advised by the Spiritual Hierarchy (the Ascended Masters) to be in control of time and space, rather than having time and space control us. Spiritual evolution, Unity Consciousness, "Light Body" status, Graduation, and Ascension are all beyond the limitations of time and space. Ascension combines the spiritual world of non-time and the physical world of time. Love is the key to helping make this combination work in harmony, since love is truly in the "Now" moment, and beyond time. Love always occurs within the "Now" moment, separate from time. When you live in the space of love, you are beyond time; there is no time but the present moment.[5]

It is in the timeless moments that envelope us when we are in love, or making love, that most humans get to experience the "Now." The sense that we are one and the feelings that come over us when we are deeply in love are totally out of time, vibrating on a much higher frequency. *That* frequency is intrinsic to and omnipresent in the Fourth Dimension; as the operative word, "love" permeates that continuum.

This is why everyone from Metatron to the Indigenous wisdom keepers keep telling us that everything we need to make it through the ascension process is inside the human heart; when we are in that place, we vibrate on a Fourth Dimensional wavelength, "in love," beyond time and space, fully connected to the Unity of life. Mother Mary seems to agree:

Humanity seems to be caught up in what comprises each dimension and how you can tell which dimension you are working with. I do not see that as germane to the question of advancement. I feel it is best to make certain one has opened up the heart structure to receive love and to give love freely. I feel that if one can do that, then arriving at the next higher dimension is assured. . . . If one cannot love, then one is lost to the process of ascending, as it is the vibrations of love that will allow entry into the next higher dimension.[6]

The man who manifested his worst fears in Drunvalo's quote would have had a completely different experience if he knew more about love and had the ability to remain centered in the moment. It pays to be informed because what we will be able to create from love sounds like it'll be way more fun than what'll happen if we take all of our fears along for the ride. Let's see what Drunvalo has to say about how it will go for those of us who manage to remain in our hearts after we come out on the other side.

That's just the beginning of course. So you are born into a new world and you survive. From this point on there are various possibilities. One that will invariably occur is that after a while you'll start to explore this reality, and at one point you will realize that whatever you think, happens.

At this point people often look down at their bodies and say "Wow," and, with their thoughts, perfect their bodies and physically become what they always wanted to be. They will heal everything, grow back arms and legs. Why not? It's like a toy to a child. Because egos often still function a little bit at this stage, you might make yourself really beautiful or handsome or taller. But you will soon get bored with perfecting your body. You will begin to explore the rest of your new reality.

One thing that will almost certainly happen; you'll suddenly notice large moving lights around the area you're in. They're called mother and father. Yes, you will have parents in the Fourth Dimension. It is, however, the last time, for in the next higher world you will not.

In the area of the Fourth Dimension where you arrive, the family problems we have experienced here on Earth don't exist. Your mother and father there will love you in ways you probably have only dreamed of on Earth. They will completely love and take care of you. They will not allow anything to happen to you in a bad way once you have survived. You have absolutely nothing to worry about. It is a time of tremendous joy if you simply surrender and allow this love to guide you. You may realize that you've won the big game of life.

All the pain and suffering you have experienced in life is over, and another beautiful and sacred level of life is emerging. Now the purpose and meaning of life begins to return consciously. You begin to experience another ancient, yet new way of being, and it's yours. It has always been yours but you gave it up.

So now you are returning to a state of awareness where God is apparent in all of life. He
is apparent with every breath that enters your
shining body of light.[7]

No pain, no lack, no war, no illness, no prejudice,
nothing but peace and harmony in a sea of unconditional love—does this sound like heaven? Do you feel
like you know what Drunvalo's talking about? I don't
know about you, but I've dreamt of these things; I've
even been there once or twice. I'm pretty sure all of us
have—and those of us who
have been fortunate enough to
experience the truest, deepest
love understand it just as well.
This is where we're going, kids;
believe it or not, we're about to
enter a realm where the fire-
flies are lit up all the time.

## Who Gets to Go?

Most of us have heard about the 144,000 chosen ones
referred to in the Bible. If we haven't read about them
in the book of Revelation, we've opened the door for
a Jehovah's Witness or two—who, as you know, are
quick to remind us that we better get right with God
and be on their bandwagon before the world comes to
an end. Reading over the biblical passage that refers to

the chosen few, one can understand why the Fundamentalists see it that way:

> Next I saw four angels, standing at the four corners of the earth, holding the four winds of the world back to keep them from blowing over the land or the sea or the trees. Then I saw another angel rising where the sun rises, carrying the seal of the living God; he called in a powerful voice to the four angels whose duty was to devastate land and sea. "Wait before you do any damage on land or at sea or to the trees, until we have put the seal on the foreheads of the servants of our God." Then I heard how many were sealed: a hundred and forty-four thousand, out of all the tribes of Israel.
>
> From the tribe of Judah, twelve thousand had been sealed; from the tribe of Rueben, twelve thousand; from the tribe of Gad, twelve thousand; from the tribe of Asher, twelve thousand; from the tribe of Naphtali, twelve thousand; from the tribe of Manasseh, twelve thousand; from the tribe of Simeon, twelve thousand; from the tribe of Levi, twelve thousand; from the tribe of Issachar, twelve thousand; from the tribe of Zebulon, twelve thousand; from the tribe of Joseph, twelve thousand; and from the tribe of Benjamin, twelve thousand were sealed.[8]

Reading through the entire book, it's quite clear that John was in a revelatory state. But aside from the fact that it sounds like he was tripping out on a tab of really good acid, one has to wonder how much of what he had to say was extracted when the Niocene Council rewrote the Bible. Even though the words in the book of Revelation attempt to tell us about the Last Days, what's left of it makes it extremely difficult to connect the dots. The only thing that *is* clear is the reference to the 144,000, and the idea that out of the three billion people who inhabit this planet, when the End Times come, only a select few will be chosen to enter the Kingdom of Heaven.

The Fundamentalists, and this includes all of the sects that approach the Bible with a "my way or the highway" perspective, narrow things down even further by saying the 144,000 will come from their lot. The Jehovah's Witnesses, the Mormons, the Baptists, the Pentecostal sects, along with the Seventh Day Adventists, and even the Catholics all believe that only *they* will be chosen. Given the fact that Christian fundamentalism is founded on fear-based dogma, that would seem to be a handicap in an unconditionally loving world. I have a feeling the ones who ascribe to those precepts will be in for a big surprise when the poles shift.

White Protestants seem to be divided when it comes to understanding what the 144,000 really refers to. The Methodists see it one way, the

Congregationalists see it another way, and the Unitarians say that it's up to each individual to decide for themselves what John actually meant when he high-lighted that magical number. Thank God I was raised in the Unitarian Church; they may be a bit too relaxed about their rituals and their dogma, but at least they let you decide for yourself how you want to relate to the things that are written in the Bible.

For what it's worth, my understanding is that the 144,000 has less to do with the number of chosen ones than it does with the number of souls that have to awaken before the Hundredth Monkey factor can kick in and open the space for all mankind to do the same. As a harmonic of the speed of light in free space, in my mind the number 144,000 is a symbolic reference to the human light body and to the Age of Light. Instead of being a hallmark of exclusion, the number refers to the idea that a critical mass of 144,000 light bodies have to be turned on and attuned to matters of spirit before human ascension can take place. It has been said that we met that quota back in the 1990s, and the ones who are already awake and aware have served as a spiri-tual vanguard; it is their inner work that has broken the ice and opened the way for the rest of humanity to ascend.

If the fundamentalist perspective leaves most of us out in the cold, the broader point of view suggests that everyone who doesn't perish during the Earth changes that attend the pole shift will complete their ascension and awaken on a whole new level. The ones who tell us *only they* will be chosen seem to forget that Christ promised to pour forth his spirit on *all* mankind. We'll all get to touch down in the Fourth Dimension, but whether we are allowed to remain will depend entirely upon each individual's ability to adapt to the laws that operate in that realm.

Once we get there, those who can't hold themselves in the "Now" and who aren't vibrating on the love frequency, will be at the mercy of their fears; just like the man who thought he needed a gun, their thoughts will manifest, and the form that they take will determine their fate. If we remember that when we are in love, there is no fear; it's easy to see why every reliable source stresses the need to tune in to that frequency and become adept at living in the "Now." As we contemplate our return to Christ Consciousness, those two things become more important than anything else.

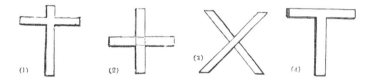

Daily synchronicities and serendipitous experiences have already shown us a little bit about how this works: being in the right place at the right time; knowing who's on the line before the phone even rings; the moment we think of something, or visualize it, it appears with no effort or expense on our part; our intuition tells us to do something and even though it seems to have no bearing on what we're involved with, we soon find out that listening to that voice pointed us in the right direction.

Once upon a time we called this coincidence or wrote it off as dumb luck, but we are learning to see that thought and manifestation are inseparable. The truth is, the little miracles that amaze us are there to show us that this is how life works; we create our experience from moment to moment and there is a direct connection between everything that happens in our external reality and what's going on inside *us*. The minute we make that connection and own the idea that the inner and outer worlds are one and the same, we touch the hem of Unity Consciousness.

These glimmers of what is to come mark the onset of changes that will expose us to levels of knowledge and existence that are as yet unknown to us. What seems miraculous to us now just so happens to be the bedrock upon which everything in the next dimension stands, and the tool that we use to restore the Kingdom to Israel will be our ability to create from within. This is why it's so important for us to see that the ascension process, and everything that goes along with it, is an open invitation to all of us to embrace our creative power and use that force to dream the new reality into being. If we wonder what life in the Fourth Dimension will be like, it is gestating inside each one of us right now, and the form that it takes will be determined by what we are able to envision.

Which gets us, once again, to the heart of the matter; how do we master the ability to manifest our visions? Is it purely a matter of thought and intent, or is there more to it? It's pretty clear that love has something to do with it too, and as we all know, love isn't a mental thing. The mind can think about love and talk about it, but that feeling is not of the mind; it lives in the heart. If this organ plays a part in the visionary process, and we are about to enter a realm where love is the operative word, I'd say it's high time we explored the heart and looked at how much it has to do with the creation process and how much it has to say about our individual and collective ability to dream up a new and better world.

This world holds pure potential for all humans. With this in mind, set about seeing in your mind what the world looks like; see green fields, beautiful clear rivers, and clean air. Now see abundance for everyone, see people smiling, happy, well fed, well cared for. See humans sharing and cooperating. What does that look like, you ask? Simply imagine it. Really see it in your mind (feel it in your heart and sense it in your body). The imagination is the paintbrush of our creations. . . . See it here and dream it into being. We will collectively see it and dream it into being.

Remember you are not alone; there are millions of us intending this new world into place.

Now put details into your dream, see all of the beauty you desire. Add color and delight. The more detailed your dream, the more tangible we make our intention. See the people of the world living in harmony not only with each other but with the planet itself. See engineering taking a turn to work with nature for the betterment of both humanity and the Earth itself, working together for the betterment of all.

See people all sharing in a plan to challenge old ideas and incorporate new, better, healthier ideas. The winds of change can be directed, and this is our opportunity to consciously choose that direction. It is a time of great gathering, a uniting of minds to create a better way, without exclusion. We can change the world. It begins with our hearts and minds.[9]

## CHAPTER 7

# The Heart

What do we know about the heart? If the mere mention of the word evokes a thousand different feelings and images, it is because the "valentine" that has come to symbolize love, pain, joy, grief, courage, and even life itself is universally understood to be the key to everything in this reality. A microcosmic image of the sun, in the human solar system, every organ in the body, including the mind, is sustained by the heart mechanism.

If we study the earliest stages of fetal development, it's quite obvious that the heart reigns supreme from the very beginning. After the first 512 cell divisions, the human fetus forms into a toroidal shape, a shape that looks a lot like a hollowed out apple, with only the central core and the outer skin to define it. This apple is the heart, or the rudimentary structure that eventually becomes the heart. Before any other part of the human body has a chance to develop, the heart is born. Out of this primordial apple, in the next series of cell divisions, our limbs, our brain, our head, and every other organ and system in the human body begin to emerge.

The Hermetic Axiom tells us that if everything about us ultimately emanates from and is sustained by the heart, there has to be a correspondence, or kinship, between *it* and the creative force that gives life to everything in the universe. If we are, in truth, a reflection of the greater whole, for us, the human heart has to be the place where God resides. Without offering too much in the way of argument, most of us would agree that what is God-like in us lives in the part of the body that poets and mystics have long referred to as the "seat of the Soul."

Recent discoveries have led the scientific community to conclude that this might be the case. They now know that the heart starts beating before the brain is even formed. According to them, this can only mean that it has its own intelligence. Their research has given rise to the theory that the heart has a brain, one that vibrates on a different level of consciousness. Unlike our "other" brain, the intelligence of the heart has nothing to do with the mind.

While the ancients and the Indigenous Elders of the world have always understood the mysteries of the heart, that knowledge was lost to everyone but them when we fell into separation. The irony of progress and what we call "civilization" is that it has taken us away from the Source. Imprisoned by belief patterns that worship the mind, the oneness that once connected us to everything is no longer part of our vocabulary. The following quote from Drunvalo Melchizedek's *Living in the Heart* tells us a little bit about what happened to the language that was once understood by everyone:

> Long, long ago, we humans were quite different. We could communicate and experience in ways that only a few in today's modern world would even begin to understand. We could use a form of communication and sensing that does not involve the brain whatsoever but rather

comes from a sacred space within the human heart.[1]

Fortunately for us, the Native People have preserved that wisdom:

In Australia, the Aborigines are still connected to an ancient web of life they call dreamtime. In this collective dream or state of consciousness, they continue to exist within their hearts and live and breathe in a world that has become almost completely lost to today's Western mind. Nearby, in New Zealand, the Maori can see across the vastness of space to the United States in their "meditations." In this manner, they link in actual communication with the Hopi to set up meetings to exchange their prophesies. Without sending a single "technological" communication, the arrangements are made. In Hawaii, the Kahuna commune with Mother Earth to ask where the fish are swimming to feed their people. The billowing white clouds in the pristine blue sky turn into the shape of a human hand that points to the teeming fish below. In a high mountain valley deep in the Sierra Nevada Mountains of Colombia, South America, lives a tribe of Indigenous people who know the language that has no words. This language comes from a sacred space within their hearts.

If only we could remember! Before Babylon, the Holy Bible says, humankind was blessed with a single language that all peoples on the Earth knew. But afterwards we were split into hundreds of spoken languages creating barriers among us, keeping us separate from one another, each in our own little introverted world.

The mistrust born of misunderstanding was our involuntary fate; in this fashion we were destined to be pitted against each other. We couldn't talk to each other. It was separation in its coldest form. Even if they were born of the same cosmic Source, brothers and sisters were unable to express their thoughts and feelings and soon became enemies. As the centuries piled upon each other, the ancient way of entering the heart to experience the common dream got lost in the isolation of the human mind.[2]

On the cusp of our return to Unity Consciousness, it behooves all of us to learn as much as we can about what the old ones understand better than anyone, because it is the secrets of the heart that hold the key to the ascension process. But before we look into the heart, it might be a good idea to examine the mind.

# Tweedledum
# and Tweedledee

The reason it's so hard to make up our minds is because the human brain has evolved in a way that divides it. Like everything else in the Third Dimension, the mind has two sides to it.

Separated by the corpus callosum, the right side of the brain governs our creative/intuitive aspect, and the left side of the brain controls our logical/linear thought processes. Female in nature, the right brain, or anima, has a totally different method of operation from the left brain, or the animus, which is fundamentally male.

It has been said that prior to the Fall, the duality that we understand to be intrinsic to the brain did not exist. There was a time when we lived in Unity

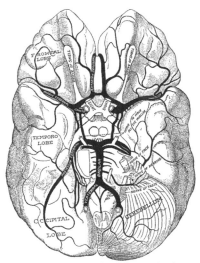

*Nerves and Arteries of the Brain. (GRAY)*

Consciousness. It was only when we fell into separation that our sense of oneness and connection became distorted by the Law of Polarity. Since that time, both the brain and the mind have become polarized to the point where we perceive everything to be separate.

Thirteen thousand years later, we are just beginning to remember that it's not that way at all. Our love affair with the power of "Now" has reminded us that we are one with all things. It has also taught us that the inner and outer worlds are, indeed, one and the same. Rediscovering a concept that didn't get much airtime prior to the sixties, in fifty years the notion that we create our own reality has taken off like a rocket.

The information systems that initially captured the popular imagination by telling us to "think and grow rich," "think off the pounds," or use the power of thought to materialize anything we could dream up, inspired many of us to take the concept one step further. If we could think about money and have it manifest, it seemed logical to conclude that we could pray for world peace and get the same result. Armed with this powerful tool, we decided that the whole idea of peaceful prayers would work even better if large numbers of meditators agreed to focus their thoughts in that direction simultaneously.

What made sense on paper didn't work out the way we intended it to. Those of us who paid attention noticed that our global peace meditations generated more wars. On April 23, 1998, thousands of people all over the world joined together in prayers for world peace. What became known as "The Great Experiment" seemed like such a good idea that it was repeated on the same date two years later. Afterwards, it became obvious to the founders of the project that even though much good came out of it, equal parts of global warfare and planetary strife seemed to be increasing at a faster rate than ever before. What was also hard to miss was the fact that the people behind the teachings that prompted us to use our creative gift to pump out money and things, even though they became incredibly rich for a time, wound up being sued in court for everything they were worth. If we thought we had the power of thought all figured out, the results of our manifestation experiments made it obvious that we were missing something very important.

Analyzing the problem, it's easy to see that the fly in the ointment might have something to do with Tweedledum and Tweedledee. When a polarized mechanism broadcasts a message, it speaks out of both sides of its mouth. If we already know that the left and the right brains are constantly at odds with one another, it doesn't take much to see that anything we wish to create with the mind will generate two equal and opposite effects. Prayers for world peace, split down the middle, will inevitably be matched with equal parts of war. Using the mind to focus our intent on *anything* guarantees that the opposite of whatever the wish contains will come into manifestation right along with it.

This is how it works in 3D. But we are ascending to the Fourth Dimension. If the Elders and the experts are correct, it won't be long before we make our transition. In a realm where thought and manifestation are simultaneous, it would be better for us if we knew exactly how that works before we arrive. So much for polarity: if we want to dream the new reality into being, we won't get very far if we keep trying to dream it up with our minds.

## The Primordial Apple

With what we know about the heart, it seems more than obvious that it is the only part of the human body that is exempt from the Law of Polarity. And while the physical organ is divided into two chambers, the beat that began in the womb is tuned to the One. Whole and complete within itself, the primordial apple contains nothing but the divine intelligence. Home to the

God within, when we make a prayer or create anything from the heart, it comes into being with no negative result. The following quote from one of the oldest books on the planet tells us a little bit about the heart space:

If someone says to you,
"In the fortified city of the imperishable,
Our body, there is a lotus
And in this lotus a tiny space:
What does it contain that one
Should desire to know it?"

You must reply:
"As vast as this space without
Is the tiny space within your heart:
Heaven and earth are found in it,
Fire and air, sun and moon,
Lightening and the constellations,
Whatever belongs to you here below,
And all that doesn't,
All this is gathered in that tiny space
Within your heart."

—CHANDOGYA UPANISHAD 8.1.2–3

What would it take to resurrect this ancient wisdom? If it has been lost to time, it hasn't been lost to everyone. The ones who understand it are everywhere, and they know how to enter the space where all things become possible. Remembering the forgotten aspect of our consciousness is important to us now because it is out of our hearts that the visions of the New Jerusalem will begin to emerge.

## The Heart Space

I first heard about the heart space back in the year 2000 at one of Drunvalo Melchizedek's Earth-Sky-Heart workshops. Already a student of his for more than two years, I was told that this workshop was going to be a little different. This was nothing new. Drunvalo's workshops were never the same and getting one's mind blown was always part of the deal—but this time, he came out with a body of information that gave new meaning to the expression.

On the fourth day of the workshop, he spent most of the day talking about the Kogi. No one in the group had ever heard of these people before, but we soon found out that of all the great Mayan tribes, the Kogi were the only ones to survive the Spanish invasions. Drunvalo told us that their ancestors escaped annihilation by retreating into the highest reaches of northern Colombia's Sierra Nevada mountain range.

Even though the Conquistadors pursued them with the intent to kill every member of the tribe, the rigors of breathing at elevations of sixteen thousand feet made it impossible for the Spaniards or their horses to chase the Kogi past a certain point; unable to catch their breath or their prey, they had no choice but to give up and surrender to the fact that the Kogi had slipped through their fingers.

If every other tribe, all of the temples and codices, and every single aspect of the Mayan culture was destroyed by the Conquistadors when they swept through South America five hundred years ago, the Kogi were the only ones left who knew anything about the sacred teachings that had been preserved by the Mayan people for close to thirteen thousand years. They were privy to a body of knowledge that was far more precious than the gold that the Spaniards had sacrificed it for, and the secrets of the heart were part of that wisdom.

Immediately prior to the workshop in question, through a strange series of events, the Kogi Elders had contacted Drunvalo to tell him that it was time for him to help them remind humanity how to return to the heart. Their message was clear. The fate of the world depended upon this, and they called upon Drunvalo because they saw in their visions that he was the only one on the planet who would be able to convey this information to the rest of humanity.

After he finished telling us why the Kogi had so much to do with the future of the human race, Drunvalo announced that we would spend the rest of the afternoon exploring the heart space. The Kogi had told him how to get there and with what his wife Claudette had taught him about the Blue School Teachings,[3] he had figured out a way to get past the complexities of the civilized mind well enough to clear the path into the heart. He understood the process; he had even gone there with one or a few other people at a time—but he had never tried it with a group this big.

Before he even began to guide us through the experience, Drunvalo told us that it's easier to get into the heart space if you're totally in the dark. After a long story about how the Kogi Mamos, the spiritual leaders of the Kogi tribe, are born and raised in complete darkness until they reach the age of twelve, Drunvalo explained that it is only in darkness that we learn to "see" with our extrasensory, or inner, vision. At that point, we all put on our blindfolds, and he took one hundred people through a process that I will share with you now.

## The Heart Process

When you do this practice, keep in mind that you are entering the imaginal realm. There is no logic here; whatever you imagine, or visualize, or see on the screen of your inner vision is real. Allow it to be. Don't let the mind judge or analyze it. If you're one of those people whose thoughts get in the way whenever you sit down to meditate, don't let that stop you. Make a deal with your mind. Tell it that you need a little peace and quiet, and in exchange for that, you will be back in an hour or two with all kinds of new and interesting things for it to think about.

## Preparation Phase

Give yourself at least an hour and arrange it so that you won't be disturbed by the phone or any other form of interruption. Sit in a chair or cross-legged on the floor, but make sure your back is straight when you do this; if you want, you can even lie down on the floor—just make sure that you don't fall asleep. Once you get settled, close your eyes, put on your blindfold, and slow your breathing down. Take long deep breaths and center peacefully into yourself.

## The Unity Breath

As you do this, begin to feel your connection to Mother Earth. Let your feelings for her fill your heart. Allow images of her beauty and feelings of love and reverence for nature to enter into the process. Sometimes it helps to feel the depth of her love by remembering that she is the one who has cared for your soul and loved you through each and every one of your lifetimes. She has always been your mother. You have always been her child.

Strengthen that connection by imagining a cord extending out from the base of your spine; picture it going down into the Earth, all the way down to the core, and see this cord attach itself to the heart of the Great Mother; let it find its way to her center.

When that connection is clear, go back into your heart, gather up all the love that you have for Mother Earth, and when those feelings become real for you, form them into a tiny little sphere. Slip the sphere into the cord (or the tube, or the root, or the beam of light, or whatever it is for you) that connects you to the Earth and let it go all the way down to the center of the Earth; feel it enter her heart and let her know how much you love her. Feel that love and give it to her.

As you continue to inhale and exhale, sense or feel the love that the Great Mother has for you and when you're ready to receive it, inhale deeply and let her love flow up from her center and allow it to enter and fill your heart. It may take a few minutes, but you will feel it, or sense it, or know it on some level of your being. Rest with this feeling until you're ready to move on to the next step.

Now bring your attention to Father Sky, the Great Spirit who watches over everything. He is the clear blue sky, the stars and the planets, the one who permeates the deepest reaches of space and governs all of the universal forces and cycles that are not of this Earth. All the angels in heaven bear his message. This awesome power is the male aspect of God. He has watched over your spirit for eons, and his love for you is as eternal and unchanging as his love for Mother Earth.

From your heart, create a line or a cord that connects you to this heavenly force; see it extend out through the top of your head, and watch it fly or float into the infinite heart of Creation. Attach it there; when the connection is secure, follow the cord back into your heart.

Gather all of the feelings of love that you have for Great Spirit. How many times has he carried you to safety? When did he ever *not* know what to do? Connect with all the things that make you feel safe, protected, and strong. What does it feel like to know that this benevolent force has always been and will always be there to support you? Whatever this feels like to you, gather all of that together, form it into a tiny sphere, and send it all the way up the cord into the heart of the Heavenly Father. Allow all of your love to merge with his limitlessness.

When this feels complete, continue breathing and connect with all the love that Father Sky has for you. When you're ready to receive it, inhale deeply, allow it to flow in from above, and feel it enter your heart; let it blend with the love of the Mother. In the place where the two become one, a child is born; that child is the God in you.

Continue to inhale and exhale, raising the Earth energies up through your spine while drawing the heavenly forces in through the top of your head. Let them meet in your heart. With every breath, feel those energies flow into your center. As you exhale feel all of that love moving out from within to touch everything in creation.

When you breathe in this way, the prana (vital energy) flow operates exactly like a pump; it flows in and out simultaneously. As each inhale meets in your center, it displaces what's there. Every time you exhale, as your breath leaves your body, the space in your heart is immediately filled by the ever-present flow of the life force. When we are centered in this flow, we are linked to the oneness that connects heaven and Earth. Now that you're there, feel yourself centered in this place of oneness for as long as you like.

The Unity Breath is a meditation in itself, and it can be used in that way; but no matter how you decide to work with it, it should always precede your entrance into the heart space. The reason for this is simple. The Unity Breath brings you to a place of balance and serves to anchor your spirit equally in both worlds. This is important because when you enter the heart, you enter the Void, and the Unity Breath stabilizes your connection to the aspect of yourself that knows how to navigate in that realm.

For me, this phase of the heart process is also the prayer, or the offering, that I make before I enter the inner sanctum. I like to be as centered as I can prior to going into the heart space, and the Unity Breath always brings me to a place of reverence for life and my connection to it. So let's imagine that we're coming from that place of oneness and move into the heart.

## Going into the Heart

Continue breathing and when you feel ready, inhale deeply, visualizing the number "3." Now exhale, through the mouth, seeing the number "3" as you watch your breath flow out like a soft mist or fog.

Inhaling again, visualize the number "2." Hold the image of the "2" as you exhale and watch your breath leave your mouth. Let it take the shape of a soft cloud or mist.

On the third inhale, see the number "1" in your inner vision. As you exhale, visualize the number "1," tall and bright, floating out on the fog that streams from your mouth.

With the next breath, enter the "1" and become part of it, or allow that energy to enter and fill every particle of your being. Continue to breathe and relax into the process.

From this place of oneness, bring your consciousness into your head. Feel what it feels like to be inside your head. Sense the skull. How does it feel? What does it look like inside your head?

When you're ready, shift your consciousness or your attention to your heart. Feel what it feels like inside your heart. How does it feel to you? What do you see there? Do you sense the difference between what it feels like to be in your head and be in your heart? If you were to put it into words, how would you describe it?

When you're ready for the next step, bring your attention back to your head. Get a sense of how it feels. Let it know that you're going to leave for a while and bring your consciousness down to your throat. Once you're there, look around. Feel your throat; get a sense of the soft tissues, look at the colors, be sensitive to the imagery that appears on the screen of your inner vision.

Spend as much time in your throat as you want. Really get a feel for it; the throat is the connection between the head and the heart. In a way, it's like the last outpost in which your consciousness prepares to transition from one world to another.

When you're ready to leave the throat, let your awareness descend down through the chest, over to the heart. This is easy to do; you can just slide right down, or you can imagine yourself in a glass elevator gliding downward toward the heart. Once you get there, stand in front of it and "see" the actual, physical organ; look at your heart. What do you see? What do you feel when you look at it? Really see your heart. It is an amazing experience to see your heart and feel the awe of knowing that it's where you came from.

When you are ready to enter it, there are two ways to get there. The Female way is easier, so I'll tell you about it first. When you choose the Female way, all you have to do is slip into the heart from any point you choose; you can just slide right in through the outer wall. If you choose the Male approach, it goes a little differently but it works just as well:

As you stand in front of your heart, "see" the energy field of light that surrounds it. Watch that field as it circulates in through the top and out through the bottom, up and around in a continuous flow. Move your attention to the top of your heart; let your consciousness float above it. Looking down, see the center point where the field of light swirls into its center. Which direction is the vortex flowing? Is it circling to the right or to the left? When you feel ready, allow yourself to fall into this vortex; let it take you into the center of your heart.

From the point of entry, whether you choose the Male way or the Female way,[4] the process is the same. When the motion stops, and you feel yourself to be in your heart space, it will probably be very dark. If it is, all you have to do is ask for the light to come or just pull the cord and turn it on. Imagine it.

When the light comes on, look around. This is your heart space. It will look different to everyone, but you will remember this place. It will seem familiar to you because you have been here many times before. This is where your soul returns between each and every one of your lifetimes.

For some people, the heart space looks like a cave; for others, it looks like a temple, or a room, or a space that is made out of earth. Everyone's heart space is different; mine looks like a three sided pyramid. When I look up, the three walls slant down to the floor.

The whole space is made out of pinkish-red stone. There's nothing in it, but I always land in the center. The only thing that's always there, sitting in the middle of this triangular stone chamber, are the coals from a burnt-out campfire.

In this place, I can dream up anything I want. When I'm there, that's what I do; or I heal things, transmute emotions, speak to my ancestors, talk to my guides, and commune with my loved ones—those at a distance and those who are on the other side. I can invite anyone or anything into this space. When it arrives, it always comes in the form of imagery, and the imagery guides me as to what to do next—because I can do anything here; nothing is beyond me—even the most difficult things are easily transmuted with the imagination.

The first time you go into your heart, get familiar with the process and explore the space for no more than half an hour. If you happen to hear a sound while you're there, don't be surprised; see if you can duplicate that sound with your voice. This will deepen your connection to the aspect of your consciousness that lives inside your heart.

## The Inner Heart

There's another aspect to the heart. It has an inner chamber. The way to this place can't be taught, but if you keep going into the heart and ask to be shown how to get there, at a certain point the way will open up.

It's hard to talk about this because there is no formal prescription for it. When Drunvalo first started to talk about it, he said that the way to the inner chamber could be found by going into the heart space and looking for the light. Following this to its source and entering into it, he said that from that point on the imagery would take you to the inner chamber. My own experience with this has shown me that the inner heart is indeed the place where *"heaven and Earth, fire and air, sun and moon, lightening and constellations"* can be found—but I can't tell you how to get there because your way will be different from mine.

## ∼ Returning to Polarity ∼

When you are ready to return to your everyday world, all you have to do is leave the heart the same way you entered it and allow your awareness to move back up to the throat. Once you're in the throat, get a sense of it. Feel yourself there. Check out the imagery and when you're done, bring your consciousness into your head. Orient yourself, make sure you're facing in the right direction, open your eyes, and bring yourself back to 3D.

### One Final Note

Some people find it difficult to enter the heart space. If you have a hard time with this process, it's because your heart holds too much pain to allow you to come in. When this is the case, it is important to work with a healer who knows how to clear those blockages. There are many healing modalities that have the capacity to heal the trauma and make room in your heart for you. Part of the heart work involves dealing with your emotional issues, when and if it becomes obvious that they inhibit your inner development.

# Where Do
# We Go from Here?

As I write these words, the tabloids are having a field day feeding off our preoccupation with the End Times; Hollywood is all over it, too. And while the media misinforms the public, the Fundamentalists go at it from a different perspective, and the New Agers spin it into something else. There are a million ways to look at the times we're in. How we choose to see them is our own business, but at this point, most of us are clear that we are living through the End of Time, and the ones who seem to know about it are the ones who tell us that no matter who we are, the heart is the only way to get from one world to another.

Within the framework of the method that we've outlined above, as you begin to explore the sacred space within the heart, your experience of it—along with the images that appear—will guide you from there. All you have to do is learn to trust what you feel or sense or see when you enter that space. The more you go into it, the more you will learn about it and the easier it will be to reawaken this ancient aspect of your consciousness.

For now, let's sit with what we've talked about so far and let it sink in. As you can guess, there's much more to say about the heart and its connection to the ascension process, but we can't talk about everything all at once. The purpose of this chapter was to introduce you to it and give you a way to get to know it a little better.

Experience is the only true teacher. Experiment; use this meditation. The heart lies at the center of it and the God in you lives there. Who knows what we could create if all of us began to live from that place?

> The purpose of awakening is to dispel the illusion of separation. Nothing else is holding back the evolution of your planet.[5]

**Author's note:** All of the information in this chapter comes from the teachings of Drunvalo Melchizedek. When it came time to write it, I went to Drunvalo to ask his permission, and he encouraged me to speak about what I have learned from him in my own words. Those of you who wish to go straight to the source will find the full instructions for the heart process in Drunvalo's book, *Living in the Heart.* The book includes a guided meditation CD that takes you through the process. For more information about Drunvalo Melchizedek and his work, go to: *www.onelotus.net* or *www.spiritofmaat.com.*

CHAPTER 8

# More about the Heart

One of the problems with human nature is our tendency to read or hear about something and assume that we know all about it. So many times I've heard people say, "I know all about the heart"—the intellectual knowing; the *idea* of it is enough for them.

There is another version of this, one that is rampant on the New Age workshop circuit that assumes that anything we take an interest in automatically becomes ours because we paid our tuition and sat through the five-day seminar. What I call the "Spiritual Big-Mac" always reminds me of something G. I. Gurdjieff once wrote about the way Americans cook chicken soup:

> Into a very commodious pot, set on the hearth, common water is poured, and then a few very finely chopped leaves of parsley are strewn into it.
>
> Then both doors of the kitchen must be opened wide, or, if there is only one door, a window must be opened wide, and, while the incantation is very loudly pronounced, a chicken must be chased through the kitchen at full speed.
>
> Upon this, a most delicious "chicken soup" is ready hot in the pot.[1]

To the Western mind, a mind that is filled with a lot of materialistic mental constructs, the biggest pitfall for anyone who decides to walk the spiritual path is the idea that the information alone is enough to unlock the door to higher consciousness. Like the chicken, we run through the kitchen and drive on through to the next workshop, collecting wisdom without allowing any of it to simmer in the cauldron of our own experience.

What we forget is that things of this nature take time, and unlike most of what we focus on, none of it can be bought. No matter how much we spend on spiritual information, the truth is that our tuition to the inner realms costs about as much as it costs a grain of sand to turn into a pearl. Time and the wish to be who we are create our connection to the heart space. Once the connection is made, layers of experience show us that each time we enter that world, our outer reality begins to reflect the imagery we dream up when we're there. Living proof inspires us to keep exploring and in the process, we evolve into a deeper understanding of what can be done from that place.

It may help you to know that I've spent nine years going into my heart, and I still don't know much about it. Mostly I go there to process questions, clear emotional blocks, and attune myself to Spirit. There is no doubt in my mind that anything can be transformed inside this sacred space—but I have realized that what I have seen is just the tip of an iceberg of possibilities and that my vision of what can be done from the heart needs to expand to include more than just me in the process. If it remains where it is, who will it serve—especially now?

Between the reality of imminent changes and the prospect of awakening on a higher level of consciousness, the heart chamber is the connecting link. And if this universal terminal is indeed the place where we can find our way through those changes well enough to bring the new reality into being, wouldn't it be wise to accept the fact that it's time to get down to the station? I'd say it's high time; as I write these words, I don't even know if this book will make it into print before the poles shift.

## Going Deeper

The process that we outlined in the previous chapter isn't the only way to get into the heart, but it happens to be the way that works for most of us. Don't deprive yourself of the opportunity to use it. Give it a chance to show you the way. As you explore this place and see how easy it is to transmute even the most difficult personal issues, it will soon dawn on you that even your worst nightmare can be transformed here. Hate turns to love, revenge morphs into forgiveness, fear becomes trust, and the answer to every question reveals itself in a way that allows you to understand what the truth is.

Over time, as the heart unifies what can't be reconciled by the mind, you begin to see that this is the "real" world and that everything in your outer reality is a reflection of it. When that happens, it becomes more than clear that you're better off living in the heart and creating your experience from that space all of the time. Why not? At first, the possibility seems out of reach, until you remember where we're going and realize that perhaps we've been guided back to the heart for a reason. If we are returning to Unity Consciousness, it would seem to be the best way to prepare for what is to come.

If layers of trauma block the entrance, it means that you're being invited to heal them. Don't take it as a sign that you're the only person on the planet who isn't allowed to access your own divinity. Consider this part of the process and deal with it. Healing emotional trauma is easy, but you can't do it alone, so find a good energy worker, someone who knows how to clear it at the cellular level, and allow them to help you process it. Once you get past all of your garbage, the path into your heart will open.

In the beginning, you will probably spend a lot of time exploring the issues that concern you in your life as you're living it now. As time goes on, those things will change and the space will open for you to expand into a broader vision of who you are and why you came here. At a certain point, you will feel and know that there is One Heart beating through everything and that each one of our hearts is part of a greater entity that unifies and supports everything in creation.

Every time we make a journey into the heart space, we strengthen our awareness of and our connection to the "One Heart," or the Unity Consciousness, that connects us all. Each attempt to enter that world allows us to understand a little bit more about who we are in relation to it. What soon becomes apparent is the sense that this is the place where heaven and Earth come together, and that it is the opening that allows us to access not just ourselves and each other but all life, everywhere.

This awareness also helps us to see exactly why life on planet Earth has gotten so out of balance. If the heart is what allows us to connect with the Source, the fact that its wisdom was lost so long ago makes it more than clear that we have been totally out of touch with the truth, the rest of the universe, and ourselves since the Fall. With the human component out of commission for that length of time, is it any wonder that the world is falling apart? As we rediscover the wisdom that sank with Atlantis, it's easy to see that the human heart and the God within each one of us hold the keys to the Kingdom of Israel.

## Suiting Up

Beyond what we know about the heart, is there anything else we can do to prepare for the ascension and ease our passage through the pole shift? Back when I first began to think about these things, I would have said, *"Head for the hills, grow your own food, know where your water is, stock up on plenty of rice and beans, pray hard, and wait it out in a sustainable dwelling."*

Part of me still feels like this is a good idea, but I've learned a few things in the last four decades, and what I see now is that going up country could be part of it, but because this is a vibrational shift, where we are at the physical level really doesn't matter. Moving through it is more about being on the right frequency than it is about being in the right location with all the right stuff. A city dweller with an open heart would have a much easier time moving through this process than a sustainability freak with a defensive attitude.

Regardless of who we are, or where we're coming from, one way or another all of us will move up to the next grid level. Those of us who aren't in attunement will die physically and be resurrected in the Fifth World. Through the Law of Resonance, the ones whose hearts are awake and vibrating on the Earth's new wavelength will ascend right along with the planet. It's that simple.

As we wait for the Great Mother to deliver herself, the best way to prepare for the shift is to do things that help you remember to go into your heart. What follows is a list of things that always work for me:

- Deepen your connection to nature
- Spend more time with the people you love
- Love your children. Let *them* teach *you* how to live

- Rest
- Dream
- Eat
- Work
- Dance
- Make music
- Hang out with animals
- Talk to the trees
- Don't answer the phone
- Listen to the birds
- Turn off the TV
- Breathe
- Feel the wind
- Pray
- Forgive
- Be truthful
- Call the Ascended Masters
- Look at the sky. Watch the clouds
- Feel the rain
- Play more
- Make love
- Swim. Take a dip in the ocean
- Watch the sun rise and set
- Stay up late and look at the stars
- Grow something
- Make something
- Lie awake at night and listen to your heart beat
- Drink a lot of water

- Hold a baby
- Be still. Hear the silence
- Talk to your body. Listen to it. Give it what it needs
- Remember the first time you felt loved, unconditionally
- Share what you have. Give it freely
- Slow down
- Keep everything really simple
- Be kind. Do your best to tolerate the weaknesses of others

It seems strange to have to tell ourselves to do these things, but that's how twisted and mechanized our lives have become. We're so busy micromanaging our time and our plans, we're totally out of touch with life and so confused by it all that we don't even remember what it means to be alive. How hard would it be for us to slow down and get real about being human?

Go down the list; everything on it is free. It costs nothing to remind yourself where the heart lies. In the course of doing any and all of the above, the cellular memory attunes to the heart resonance and the spirit remembers where it came from. These little acts of love will spill over into your outer reality in ways that help you remember how to live. This is just as important as it is to keep the heart open; because if we don't even know how to live in this world, what makes us think we're ready to move on to the next one?

# Meditation

One of the best ways to slow down and enter into the moment is through some form of meditative practice. There are a million ways to do it. Those of you who can't make it happen in stillness can use your body to connect with spirit. Walking can be a meditation. You can do it just as easily with yoga or chi gung or tai chi. Dancing around the kitchen works, too. Active meditations are good for people who think too much. If you want to go a little further with it, build a labyrinth in your backyard and walk it every day. Moving through the circuits of a Seven Turn labyrinth is one of the oldest known ways to connect with Spirit.

No matter how we approach it, the act of centering ourselves in meditation brings us to a still point that allows us to return to the inner self. From that place, it's easier to live in the present, and it's easier to engage with life in a way that makes it possible to bring more soul into all of our activities. No longer functioning through the mask of the personality, the spirit comes through with no interference.

This change of state has as much of an impact on the conditions in our outer reality as it does on us. In the same way that a pebble thrown into a still body of water forms concentric rings that ripple out forever, whenever we meditate, the light in us expands beyond the limits of our own energy field, illuminating everything in its path. This radiance has a vibration; when we are centered in it, that energy has an uplifting effect on whomever or whatever we come into contact with.

As far as the various meditative techniques go, what works for one person doesn't work for another. The point isn't how you get there; it's more about your relationship to the practice and the sincerity of your wish to engage in it. If you want to eliminate the guesswork, start out with the Unity Breath that we outlined in chapter 7. Every ancient and Indigenous spiritual tradition has its own version of this meditation. There is a good reason for this. The Unity Breath is one of the oldest meditative methods on the planet and it has withstood the test of time because it works.

## The Mer-Ka-Ba and the Mer-Ka-Ba Meditation

The Mer-Ka-Ba and the meditation that gets it spinning could use a chapter, or perhaps even a book, of their own. The information system that surrounds those teachings is an enormous body of work, one that a quick trip through the proverbial "kitchen" could never do justice to. At the same time, there's no way to address the question of "What more can we do?" without talking about the Mer-Ka-Ba.

Since we can't take the time to cover it all, I am including a brief overview of the Mer-Ka-Ba material and a little bit about the meditation itself, because for anyone who wants to be well prepared for the ascension, it is essential to have a basic understanding of what they are. If, after reading this section, you wish to explore the information in more depth, I encourage you to check out Drunvalo Melchizedek's books, tapes, and workshops; they are the best source for all of that material. They can be accessed at *www.onelotus.net, www. drunvalo.net,* or *www.floweroflife.com.*

If love is the fuel and the heart is the engine, the Mer-Ka-Ba is the vehicle that transports us from one world to another. Otherwise known as the Light Body, or the ascension vehicle, ancient Hebraic texts refer to it as the "Chariot" that carries the soul to the "Throne of God."

For those of you who are unfamiliar with the term, the Mer-Ka-Ba is the name for the star tetrahedronal energy field that surrounds the human body. Universally understood to be the geometric blueprint that allows Spirit to both contain itself in a form and move freely between dimensions, the Mer-Ka-Ba is the Spiritual template for everything in creation; it is, thus, a vital part of the ascension process.

The Mer-Ka-Ba traditions can be traced all the way back to Atlantis. The centerpiece of antediluvian spirituality, like so many other things, the traditions went underground after the Fall. As we spiraled down into the dark half of the Grand Cycle, that knowledge was forgotten for thousands of years, along with the secrets of the heart, but it never completely disappeared. Kept alive by the ones who were chosen to preserve them, the Mer-Ka-Ba teachings resurfaced in Egypt during the reign of Akhenaton. It was he who reestablished the traditions in what became known as the Left and the Right Eye of Horus Mystery Schools.

If Akhenaton went down in history as one of the bad guys, all I can say is, so much for history. When you sweep the dust off what remains of the story, you soon find out that he was a fully enlightened, immortal being whose efforts to preserve the truth were viciously undermined by a corrupt priesthood. Known to have instructed initiates in the ascension mysteries, during his lifetime Akhenaton was able to bring three hundred people (most, if not all, of whom were women) into Christ Consciousness.

That he actually succeeded in awakening three hundred human beings to their birthright created a conflict of interest with the rich and powerful priests, who knew they would have to give up everything if the masses caught on to the fact that they could access the divine on their own. Akhenaton and his mysteries posed such a threat to their priestly position and their need to keep the people in the dark, that they did him in with a dose of poison, duped the historians into casting him as a villain, and, while they were at it, disposed of the Mer-Ka-Ba wisdom once and for all—or so they thought.

A little over three thousand years later, in 1985, those teachings were returned to us through the work of Drunvalo Melchizedek. Well known as the disseminator of the Flower of Life teachings, Drunvalo has spent twenty-five years traveling the world, sharing the original Mer-Ka-Ba information and the meditation that goes along with it with thousands of people all

*The Weiser Field Guide to Ascension*

over the planet. He has done more to prepare humanity for the ascension process than most, and the dissemination of the Mer-Ka-Ba meditation was and is a major part of that effort.

The Light Body, or the Mer-Ka-Ba field, can be easily reactivated through the practice of the Mer-Ka-Ba Meditation. This method incorporates seventeen breaths, taken in a specific way, along with mudras (hand positions) that serve to reactivate the Mer-Ka-Ba field and restore the connection to the Higher Self. The practice also balances the Male and the Female aspect and brings the Spirit into alignment with the mind and the body.[2]

Understanding the Mer-Ka-Ba and reactivating the Light Body are important to us now because the Mer-Ka-Ba Field resonates with all frequencies, earthly and otherwise. When it is reinstated, it serves to insulate, shield, or protect the Spirit, regardless of what goes on around it. Spinning at nine-tenths the speed of light, this star tetrahedronal "Chariot" is like a virtual spacesuit; when we reconnect with it consciously, it's as if we become the occupant of a crystalline vehicle that can operate in any dimension.

Back in chapter 5, when we went over the phases of the pole shift, we talked about how important it is to activate the Mer-Ka-Ba at the onset the preliminary breakdown phase that occurs right before the magnetic poles cut loose. The reason for this is simple. When the magnetic field collapses and the thick granite sub-layer dissolves, all the memories of everything that ever took place on the planet are erased; and because each one of us is a microcosmic replica of the Earth, all of *our* memories disappear as well.

According to the Indigenous Elders, most of the problems that assail people during a pole shift are caused by the fact that when the magnetic field goes down, if we don't know what's going on, we literally lose our minds. With no reference point for anything, and no memory of who we are or what anything is, the pole shift aspect of the ascension process becomes a much more complex and dangerous ordeal.

Because the Mer-Ka-Ba Field is tuned to the Earth's frequency, whatever that happens to be, whenever she shifts to a new frequency, the Light Body automatically adopts that resonance. This allows the Chariot to carry the physical body through the pole shift and on to the next level with everything, including the memory, intact. With the memory retained and a solid sense of what's taking place, it's easier to move through the ascension process and arrive in the Fifth World with a clear sense of who you are, where you came from, and what you're doing in the new reality.

I've never had the opportunity to see if my Mer-Ka-Ba Field would stand up to the rigors of a pole shift, but it has protected me in enough hairy and/or toxic situations for me to have no doubt that it could. Time will tell. My preoccupation with the prospect of ascension has spurred a deeper interest in the Mer-

Ka-Ba and a deeper wish to practice the meditation. Regardless of what form of meditation you engage in, consider learning the Mer-Ka-Ba Meditation and include it in your daily practice. There is plenty of evidence to suggest that it will save more than your memories down the road a piece.

Before we leave the subject, there's one more thing you need to know about the Mer-Ka-Ba: it can't be activated without the heart. The two are intimately entwined and both of them have too much to say about the ascension process for us to ignore their connection. The following quote tells us why one can't exist without the other:

> Simply becoming involved with the technical relationships of the Mer-Ka-Ba, such as correcting our breathing patterns or mentally realizing the infinite connections to all patterns of life, for example, is not enough. At least one other factor is even more important than the Mer-Ka-Ba itself, and that is the understanding, realization, and living of divine love. For it is divine love, sometimes referred to as unconditional love, that is the primary factor that allows the Mer-Ka-Ba to become a living field of light.[3]

If you choose to learn the Mer-Ka-Ba Meditation, you need to understand that taking the breaths and going through each step won't be enough to reactivate the Light Body. That energy field is alive and it is the human heart that gives it life. The inner wish to reconnect with the Christ within you and the love that you feel for everything in creation has to fill every breath—because like we said in the beginning: if love is the fuel and the heart is the engine, it's what we feel in our hearts that drives the Chariot and gets the Mer-Ka-Ba spinning.

If you take anything from this chapter, I hope it inspires you to go into your heart and deepen your connection to the terminal through which everything in creation is accessible. Whatever comes, the only way to prepare for it is by going to the place within yourself that knows exactly what to do. From that place you will come to understand the purpose of your own life and the full extent to which all of us are creators here.

I have long held the feeling that if everyone could enter that world and from this imaginal realm learn how to envision a new reality, we could move through the ascension process and everything it entails in a conscious way, joyously anticipating a rebirth instead of fearing death and destruction. Consider the heart; don't make this a quick trip through the kitchen. It is the most important aspect of the ascension process. Next to it, you will find the Mer-Ka-Ba; if you want to make the most of this experience, take it into consideration as well.

## CHAPTER 9

# Sex and the Ascension

It was Wilhelm Reich who told us that all the problems in the world are genitally based. That he managed to prove it didn't go over too well with the powers that be. After they incarcerated him for blowing the lid off the function of the orgasm, in 1956, in one of the worst cases of governmentally sanctioned censorship in history, several tons of Reich's publications were burned by the FDA. Less than a year later, the free-energy genius died in the Lewisburg Pennsylvania Penitentiary of what many claim was an artificially engineered heart attack.

When you look at what's left of his research, it's hard to figure out why they went to such great lengths to suppress it. Reich's discoveries revealed quite simply that the God Force is held in the orgasm, and that our relationship to it and our sexuality has been distorted by artificial religious and cultural belief patterns that prevent us from accessing that aspect of ourselves. According to Reich, the sexual/spiritual connection disappeared when the church put a lock on our genitals. As a result, what we call our lesser urges have been diverted into channels that are filled with frustration, violence, pornography, pedophilia, and/or the more benign but equally perverse manifestation of no sex at all.

Someone please tell me: why would coming up with the theory that sex serves a spiritual purpose invite a prison sentence, a massive book burning, and a visit from murder incorporated? If God can be found in an orgasm, why have we been sold the notion that the act of making love is sinful, dirty, bad, and/or the work of the Devil? What is it about sex that caused the powers that be to destroy the man who resurrected its secrets, and why are those secrets important to us now?

Before we can talk about sex and its relationship to the ascension process, we need to erase the blackboard and eighty-six everything we've been told—original sin, guilt and shame, only for procreation—all of it. Those of us who think we got over that stuff ages ago may be better prepared for this conversation than a recovering Catholic or Born Again Christian, but keep an open mind. Like everything else in this world, there's always more to know about it, and the outer limits of the sexual sphere are certainly no exception.

## Dr. Ruth

If we haven't been completely sucked in by our religious programming, there's a good chance that we enjoy sex and have a healthy relationship to that aspect of our lives. And unless we're involved in certain Tantric practices, when we have an orgasm, we release that energy into the universe without thinking too much about what it is or where it's going. For most of us, sexual ecstasy feels good, and that's all there is to it; but according to Drunvalo, the orgasm is more than just a pleasant physical sensation:

> Sex, and specifically the orgasm, is more
> than just something that feels good and allows

procreation. There are many other functions, such as the release of dysfunctional energy within the body, which can help to keep one from becoming diseased. There is the function that opens the higher chakras, and under the right conditions allows a person to begin the process of enlightenment. And further, if two people, lovers, practice sacred sex, the entire experience can lead them together into higher consciousness and into worlds beyond this plane.[1]

Who knew? If you're wondering why the Christian traditions are filled with precepts that tell us sex is Lucifer's domain, it's because for more than two thousand years that belief system has been controlled by forces whose vested interests are more concerned with keeping humanity asleep than they are with turning us on to the truth. When Wilhelm Reich rediscovered the function of the orgasm, he wandered into classified territory, blowing the doors off one of the best-kept secrets of all time. Underneath all the Christian admonitions, what we never knew about sex has deterred us from awakening to the fact that beyond serving as a release mechanism, it is one of the best ways to connect with Spirit. The following quote tells us a little bit about what happens to our sexual energy when we *don't* work with it consciously:

Most people in the world are ignorant about what happens to their sexual energy after they have an orgasm. Usually, the energy moves up the spine and out the top of the head directly into the eighth or the thirteenth chakra (same chakra, different system). In a few rare cases, the sexual energy is released down the spine into the hidden center, below the feet, the point opposite the one above the head. In either case, the sexual energy—the concentrated life force energy called prana in Hinduism—is dissipated and lost. It is similar to discharging a battery into a ground wire. It is no longer in the battery and so it is gone forever. This is what all the Tantric systems that I am aware of believe, that orgasm brings one a little closer to death because a person loses his or her life-force energy in the orgasm and is made weaker. But the Egyptians found long ago that it does not have to be this way.[2]

All of the ancient spiritual traditions have a Tantric component. Many of them instruct the male to avoid ejaculating. The Hindu, the Tibetan, and the Chinese Taoist Tantra systems all advise the male to withhold the orgasm in a way that moves the life force energy into the higher spiritual centers. The Egyptian Tantra system understood the orgasm to be both healthy and necessary, and their way of approaching the sexual mysteries did not include having the male refrain from releasing his sperm.

Within that body of information is a practice that allows one to move the orgasm up the spine, out the back, over the head, and into the heart chakra, in a way that rejuvenates the body, mind, and spirit and doesn't require the male to contain himself. Known as "ankhing," this method of experiencing orgasm returns the life force to the heart center and reinvigorates the Spirit. It was held by the Egyptians to be one of the keys to immortality.

The name of the practice derives from the symbol that we see so often we take it for granted. New Age emporiums are filled with jewelry and spiritual trinkets that capitalize on the power we give to the ankh. Also known as the Egyptian Cross, the textbooks tell us it is the symbol for eternal life, but they fail to tell us why. When you dig deep enough to find out what it really meant to the ancient Egyptians, eventually you discover that the ankh is the template for the channel that carries the orgasm up the spine and allows us to move that energy back into the body.

Like every other human feature, all of us come fully equipped with an ankhing tube. When we become conscious of it and start to use it, it opens up. For those of you who wish to experiment with this practice, included here are the instructions for the Egyptian

Orgasm. This information first appeared in an article that was written by Drunvalo for the April 2001 edition of the *Spirit of Ma'at* magazine entitled "Ancient Egyptian Sexual Ankhing":

### Instructions for the Egyptian Orgasm

Here is exactly how to achieve the *ankhing* associated with the human orgasm. Whatever you do sexually before the orgasm is completely up to you. I am not here to judge you—and definitely the Egyptians would not, since they believe in knowing all sixty-four sexual modes before you enter the King's Chamber to ascend to the next level of consciousness. This is their idea, but it is important to know that it is not necessary. You can reach the next level of consciousness without knowing this information. However, from their point of view, the idea of *ankhing* is of paramount importance in achieving eternal life. You will have to decide for yourself if it is something you wish to practice.

1. The moment you feel the sexual energy about to rise up your spine, take a very deep breath, filling your lungs about 9/10th full; then hold your breath.
2. Allow the sexual energy of the orgasm to come up your spine. But at the moment it reaches the fifth chakra (located just a couple of finger widths above

the sternum), with your willpower you must turn the flow of sexual energy 90 degrees out the back of the body. It will then automatically continue inside the *ankh* tube. It will slowly turn until it passes through the eighth (or thirteenth) chakra, one hand-length above the head at 90 degrees to the vertical. It will then continue to curve around until it returns to the fifth chakra, where it began, only this time in front of the body.

Even if you don't understand what was just said, it will happen automatically if you get it started out the back of the body at the fifth chakra, and it will automatically come back around to the front of the body and reconnect at the fifth chakra. You just have to make it turn 90 degrees so that it begins.

3. It will often slow down as it approaches the point of origin, the fifth chakra. If you can see the energy, it comes to a sharp point. When it approaches the fifth chakra from the front of the body, there is sometimes a tremendous jolt as it reconnects with this chakra again. All this takes place while you are holding your first breath.

4. The instant the sexual energy reconnects with its source, the fifth chakra, take in the full breath. You had filled your lungs only 9/10th full, so now you fill your lungs as completely as you can.

5.  Now exhale very, very slowly. The sexual energy will continue on around the *ankh* channel as long as you are exhaling. When you reach the bottom of this breath, you will continue to breathe very deeply, but a change happens here.

6.  It is here that, if you know the Light Body work of the Mer-Ka-Ba, you would begin to breathe from the two poles using the Mer-Ka-Ba breathing. [He is referring to the spherical breathing method that we outlined in the Unity Breath.] But if you are like most people and don't know this work, then continue to breathe deeply until you feel the relaxation spread throughout your body. Then relax your breath to your normal rate. Feel every cell becoming rejuvenated by this life-force energy. Let this energy reach down into the deepest physical levels of your body structure even past the cellular level. Feel how this beautiful energy surrounds your very being and brings health to your body, mind, and heart.

7.  Once the relaxation begins, slow your breath down to a normal shallow breathing.

8.  If possible, allow yourself to relax or even sleep for a while afterward.

If you practice this for even one week, I believe you will more than understand. If you practice it continually, it will begin to give health and strength to your mental, emotional, and physical bodies. It will give great strength and power to your Light Body as well.

If for any reason this practice does not feel right, stop and return to normal. It just is not time. . . .

You can talk about it all day, but if you try it one time, you will understand. However, it is not easy to do it in one test. For the first few times, the sexual energy will often shoot out past the point of the fifth chakra and continue on up and out of the body. So it takes practice. Once it is learned, I doubt seriously if you would ever have an orgasm any other way. It's too powerful and it feels too good. Once your body remembers this experience, it is not likely to revert back to the old way.[3]

## Where Were We?

Why do we need to know this? What does it have to do with ascension?

We've talked about activating the Mer-Ka-Ba and how important it is to reconnect with the Light Body. By now we understand the importance of meditation and prayer as well. And it's easy to see why deepening the inner connection makes a difference because we know that the heart is the key to the ascension process. But no transformation is complete until we experience it at the cellular level, and the ankhing method of achieving orgasm awakens the God in our cells, allowing the physical vehicle to enlighten itself.

When every cell in the body is awake, it serves to support the wishes of the Spirit and opens the mind in ways that allow the consciousness to expand beyond its limits. It's as if the physical vehicle becomes an active participant in the process or the embodiment of what we mean when we refer to it as the "Temple of the Soul." In restoring the life-force energy to the heart center, the ankhing practice keeps the body enlightened and able to hold the higher frequencies that get beamed into the heart and the mind whenever we go within.

Our preoccupation with sex never had a better excuse to turn its attention away from the programming that has kept it focused on everything but its ultimate purpose. I often wonder what would happen if everyone knew about the ankhing method. What if, instead of draining the battery with every orgasm, we channeled that energy into our hearts? Would it make a difference? I know one thing: it would definitely make whatever's going on in the bedroom much more interesting.

Which gets us to another thing: the statistics indicate that our love making is on a down swing. With all the wholesale sex pouring out of the media, you'd think the opposite would be true, but it isn't that way at all. Is this sexual ennui due to the fact that someone forgot to mention the spiritual component? Did it ever occur to us that there might be one? I have a feeling no one's in the bedroom because without that element, pretty much everything loses its meaning.

This is what Wilhelm Reich meant when he said that it is our artificial belief constructs that prevent us from accessing the power inherent in the orgasm. Between religious injunctions that tell us sex is only permissible within the sanctity of marriage and the soft porn blaring off the movie screens, our sexual instincts are completely controlled by a system that has no interest in having anyone know the truth. If you think this is stretching it, ask yourself this: why do they tantalize us with hardcore sex and leave us to live with the conflict that surfaces when we shut off the DVD player and have to wrestle with beliefs that make us feel guilty for even watching the show? Within this catch-22, our head trips have us so confused about sex, unraveling its secrets would seem to be the only way out.

If the life-force energy that is rightfully ours has been misappropriated by those who don't want us to connect with it, with the ascension process so near at hand, could we take it upon ourselves to reclaim ownership of our Spirit and begin to work with our sexuality in a conscious way? Now that we know a little bit about the Egyptian orgasm, hopefully we can use that information, along with the heart process, the Mer-Ka-Ba Meditation, the Unity Breath, and our desire to remember how to be alive in this world, as a network of mutually supportive practices that fine-tune us for our entrance into the Age of Light.

# CHAPTER 10

# The Ascension Letters

A few chapters ago, we spoke about the Kogi without elaborating too much on anything but the fact that they have come forward with a body of information that could have a major impact on the fate of the world. If you recall, we talked about how they were the only members of the Mayan Nation to survive the Spanish invasions, and that because of this, they have been the keepers of secrets and traditions that would have been lost forever if they hadn't managed to escape. By itself, that story is amazing; but the whole story is even more so.

The Kogi Elders tell us that that their ancestors were once the High Priests of Atlantis, members of an inner circle known as the Naccal Mystery School. Masters of wisdom, the Naccals used their abilities to maintain balance and harmony here on Earth and to help keep mankind attuned to the ways of Nature.

When Atlantis sank beneath the waves, the Naccals, along with members of the outer circle whose descendants are now Mayan or Native American, escaped the deluge in boats that carried them to the eastern shores of the Americas. For approximately 12,500 years, the Kogi Mamas and the Mayan and Native American Elders lived in a way that allowed them to preserve the wisdom that was understood by everyone prior to the Fall.

Five hundred-odd years ago, all of that knowledge would have been completely destroyed were it not for those who have kept it safe in the oral traditions of both the North and South American tribespeople since that time. In spite of what we think we know about them, the truth is, the Indigenous Elders haven't spoken out about anything in more than five hundred years. Others have told us about their history and their ways by patching together remnants of a past that they know nothing about—but the Elders have only really begun to come forward in the last decade, and their reasons for doing so were precipitated by the times we're in and more specifically by something the Kogi Mamas saw in their visions back in 1999.

## A Little Background

Before we get into the story, it will help you to know a little bit about the Kogi Mamas. Also known as the "Elder Elders" of the Mayan Nation, the Mamas are the High Priests of the Kogi Tribe. Revered by their people as superhuman entities, their consciousness is part of the Earth's consciousness, and their spiritual abilities are directed at making sure that Mother Earth, or *"Aluna,"* is maintained in a state of perfect health. The Kogi believe that without the Mamas, the planet would die.

From the time they are in the womb, it is known that these special individuals are the ones who are destined to be the tribal wisdom keepers. In some instances, a Mama is identified after their birth, but either way, their training begins as soon as they are recognized. The following quote from Drunvalo's book *Living in the Heart* talks about what happens to a Kogi Mama the moment they enter this world:

> What is incredibly interesting is that when a baby who is or will become a Mama is discovered within the Kogi tribe, it is taken to an unusual place for special training and upbringing. In the old days, this was a completely dark cave, but today the baby is taken to a special building constructed of all-natural materials where no light can enter. In almost complete darkness, this special baby will be fed only white foods while it grows up and given just enough light so as not to go blind. The baby also receives a most unusual spiritual training. For nine years, this baby remains in complete darkness, learning to see without using the eyes, just like the super psychic children[1] who

are emerging around the world. At nine years of age, the young child is brought out into the light to learn how to see with the eyes.[2]

Their spiritual training continues after they leave the darkness, but before they learn about anything else, the Mamas learn about the inner realms; unlike us, they begin their lives in the heart. Connected to Source, their consciousness evolves in ways that allow it to move anywhere, and the Mamas develop the ability to see and be anywhere in the world without having to leave their home. What none of us ever knew is that generations of Kogi Elders have watched over the Earth from the highest mountains of northern Colombia; despite any doubt we may have about it, it is they who have kept her spinning.

If their supernatural abilities allow them to see and be anywhere, they also endow the Mamas with the gift of prophecy, and this is where the story really begins; because for thirteen thousand years, the Kogi Mamas have never been wrong about any of their predictions, and when the one they made in 1999 didn't come to pass, it confounded them enough to go looking for a reason why.

## Story Time

In their visions, the Mamas could see that the Earth was in a near-death state as early as 1990. Because of this, they decided to extend themselves to the outside world in an attempt to warn us and inspire us to change our ways before things got any worse. Those efforts resulted in a documentary film that was produced by the BBC entitled *The Elder Brothers Warning: The Message from the Heart of the World*. Aired in 1990 and still available on video, the film opened many of our eyes, but it didn't circulate widely enough to have an impact.

Less than a decade after the BBC introduced them to us, the Mamas could see that Aluna was in a state of emergency and that she would surely be dead by or before August 11, 1999; all of their visions confirmed this. When August 11 came and went without a tremor, the Mamas went into their hearts to see what it was that had kept their prediction from coming true. Drunvalo's account of the story tells us exactly what happened:

> According to the Kogi Mamas, by the last solar eclipse of the twentieth century, on August 11, 1999, all the techno-cultural peoples of the world should have gone to another dimension of the Earth's consciousness, leaving behind the indigenous and natural peoples of the world to inherit the physical planet. (This is reminiscent of the Bible's words that the "meek shall inherit the Earth." This prediction is also very similar to what Edgar Cayce, the "sleeping prophet," said, that by the winter of 1998, the

poles of the Earth would shift and an enormous change would happen on Earth. Many New Age people thought this meant that most of the consciousness of the world would move into the Fourth Dimension.)

The young man [who relayed this information to Drunvalo] moved closer to me as if to emphasize what he was about to tell me. He lowered his voice and whispered, "On August 12, 1999, the Kogi Mamas saw that we, the techno-culture, were still here on Earth. They went into a deep meditation to see why, since this was the first time in their long history that one of their predictions didn't come true."

According to him, there in the darkness the Kogi Mamas could see lights all over the surface of the planet—and they had not been there before. In investigating these lights, the Mamas found that they were the lights of people who had learned about their Light Bodies, which in ancient times were called Mer-Ka-Bas. It was the Mamas' belief that these people with their Light Bodies had changed the course of history.

As a teacher of the science of the Mer-Ka-Ba, I know that once we remember our Mer-Ka-Ba, we can, with certain training, alter the external world by what we think and feel. According to the Kogi Mamas, some of us did change the outer world so much that a new reality was created.[3]

Out of gratitude for the work that Drunvalo has done, the Mamas sent a gift along with the emissary who showed up mysteriously at the end of a workshop to deliver their message. After he finished telling Drunvalo what they had seen, the young man handed him a small bundle of tobacco wrapped in red felt and said: "The Kogi Mamas wish to thank you for teaching about the Mer-Ka-Ba and for changing the world in the process."[4]

Ever since I was a kid, in and around all the other things that have filled up my life, my main focus has always been my spiritual work. After forty years on a path that began in earnest when I was a teenager, I didn't come across Drunvalo's work until 1997. Since that time, the Mer-Ka-Ba Teachings have been my spiritual mainstay. Every time I meditate, I see how it changes the conditions in my outer reality, and I have always held the faith that the work that I do inside myself has an impact on the greater whole. It wasn't until the Kogi story came to my attention that I had any concrete evidence to prove that my meditations were more than just a way to make my own life better.

The network of lights that the Kogi saw stretched out across the planet is made up of thousands of people. All of them are connected by the same wish and, along with the Mer-Ka-Ba Meditation, all of them understand the secrets of the heart. If it amazes you that a small percentage of the human population could do that much to change the world, try to imagine what we could do if all of us turned our attention toward the teachings of the heart. Does the Kogi story call up a desire to turn on your light? With the ascension process so clearly imminent, does anything else matter?

## The Letters

When I am not writing books, it is my good fortune to be the editor of Drunvalo's web-zine, the *Spirit of Ma'at*. Available online since the year 2000, the *Spirit of Ma'at* is a resource for people who have an interest in spiritual development and who wish to stay informed regarding the changes that are about to take all of us through the Eye of the Needle. Most, if not all, of our readers are followers of Drunvalo's work.

In the five years that I have been part of the magazine, the Great Shift has been the main point of interest. Between our office conversations and the articles that come in every month, the ascension process has generated enough speculation for me to see that in spite of all the books and courses that have attempted to enlighten us on the subject, we still don't have a grip on it. When the Blue Star appeared in the fall of 2007, and the Elders began to come forward with the last of their prophecies, I realized that the ascension question was no longer one of those things that we could afford to stay up all night and theorize about; if we had any confusion, it was time to get on the ball and clear it up.

Knowing that most of our readers practice the Mer-Ka-Ba and work with the heart process, it occurred to me that they had to be thinking about these things and that their insights might loan some clarity to the situation. I knew that my own meditations were revealing bits and pieces of information. If others were having similar experiences, it seemed to me that an open discussion would flesh out a bigger portion of the truth.

It was out of that brainstorm that we decided to devote the March 2008 edition of the *Spirit of Ma'at* to the ascension question. It turned out to be a big one. More people took it upon themselves to contribute to the "Ascension Issue" than any previous edition of the magazine. The heart of the issue was contained in an article entitled "Ascension Letters from Our Readers," a compilation of letters from people all over the world responding to the question: *Ascension, what is it?*

Reading through each letter, it seemed to me that any confusion we had prior to 2008 had miraculously cleared up. Not only were people thinking about the ascension, they were preparing for it and, in the process, acquiring a deeper sense of what it might be. At first this blew me away, until I realized that if these people were the lights that the Kogi had seen, their inner work had to be informing them about things that weren't covered in the ascension manuals.

Since we're all here to learn as much as we can, I thought it might be good to hear from someone other than myself, just to give you a sense of what others are thinking and feeling about changes that the Elders tell us are due to come to pass two years sooner than expected. The letters that follow are just some of the hundreds that we received back in the spring of 2008. They were written by people like you. Each one contains a portion of the light that the Kogi saw beaming so clearly in 1999.

*Dear Spirit of Ma'at,*

*This morning while taking time to pray and meditate, I reached an understanding that for me was profound. There are so many teachers, books, etc., available to us that we sometimes lose track of* what's important. "Know thyself, trust thyself, have faith that we are guided from our highest good" have become in my opinion the only way to understand this concept of Ascension.

It occurs to me that all the books, seminars, teachers, and sharing of ideas doesn't really matter anymore. We have come so far in so short a time. No one can give us the answers we are seeking because they are not outside of ourselves. You can't find them in a book or seminar. To find these answers at this point on the journey in our lives, all we need to do is live consciously. To live from the inside out, following the guidance within and being aware of what we create: Consciously observing that which we create, moving through time towards our highest ideas and very gently, quietly living in this way we will "Ascend."

When we get caught up in the word, we lose all understanding of what this action "Ascension" means. I feel this "Ascension" everyone is talking about will be different for each person and will be experienced differently based on the soul's highest good. I also feel that the diversity we see around us mirrors the possibilities of each individual's diversity in the experience of "Ascension." To me, this is a profound way of thinking and brings much relief of spirit. It places the life experience on the individual's trust, faith, and love of self.

We don't have to drive ourselves crazy trying to understand literally what "Ascension" is or means.

*To my understanding, we are always in some way
ascending and that this is not some new process or
some final event we are about to experience: it's only
that some of us have awakened to the fact that something is happening, some movement, and we label it
(judge it) according to our individual understanding.
The fact that we are awakening to this movement
allows us to believe that "Ascension" is something
unusual or a possible future event.*

*I truly feel that all we need to do at this point is
live consciously, seeking out our highest good and the
good of all concerned and rest in the knowledge that
we are in the loving hands of Great Spirit.*

*With Love,
Belinda*

*Dear Spirit of Ma'at,*
    *The established meaning of ascension is to move
upward or change levels, commonly understood as
achieving a level beyond or "better" than the previous
level.*
    *In the world of spiritual marketing, ascension
refers to some kind of enlightened state that trans-
forms our confused, painful, and often mundane
human experience to an experience closer to what
we have decided is "god-like"; a better and wiser
incarnation of our current situation where the idiocy*

and the acts of other humans no longer affect us—
we're above it.

True ascension is a physical act of particle
acceleration which is ignited through our chakra
system, resulting in the pineal gland activation. The
human is able to control the amounts of DMT that
are excreted which causes us to be able to inter-act
inter-dimensionally. The pineal gland acts as the
particle accelerator, which physiologically changes the
vibration and frequency of the human body. When a
person reaches an advanced stage of particle acceleration and is able to change the frequency of their cellular vibration, they can transform the physical body
so that it loses its dense atomic mass and instead
radiates through its photon particles—light.

Thanks,
Amy Reynolds, VP
Climb On! Products, Inc.

*Dear Spirit of Ma'at,*
I believe the ascension process is well begun. As
of December 2007, I've noticed that thoughts and
desires manifest very quickly, mind to mind communication has increased exponentially regardless
of distance, like-minded people are being drawn together in groups, etc. Many years ago I saw this time
as one in which secrets would be a thing of the past as

minds communicate directly. The implications of this are frightening at first, causing much chaos, but will shake out eventually. The end result will be peace.

These physical changes, among many others, are reflective of the raising of the soul vibrations of those who remain incarnate, including universal direct connection with our Space Brothers. What an exciting time to be here in a body! Choices are being made daily either to raise one's vibration or to slide into lower vibrations. The result of the choice to raise one's vibration results in movement into the 4th dimension, which is what's happening right now. There is so much more happening; it's hard to put into words.

Blessings,
Rael

Dear Spirit of Ma'at,

I think there are many ways to define ascension. Perhaps it is different for everyone. I feel I do understand it, but I have a hard time explaining it in words. It seems to be a concept that is hard to define. But I think it is a return to the beginning, then that beginning changes in and of itself each time around. It is a process that is ongoing, moving through each lifetime towards ascension by way of enlightenment and experience. We are always in a state of ascension, however to get to the nitty gritty of it, I believe *it is when your enlightenment, love, and knowledge reach a level that you become a master of life and death and the universe around you. You break through the wall of this level and move on to the next. When you reach that understanding, you fully realize that you are made of light and are able to take the form of light at will. We are all made of light and most of us know that. Our bodies are light vibrating at a lower frequency. When our enlightenment increases, so does our vibrational rate; it continues to increase until one day our bodies reach the level our spirits are at and we become pure light. But even once we have reached that state of pure light, there are different levels of that light, different phases of ascension until we become one as a species, like Ra of Venus. Then inevitably all species will become one with each other and the universe will return to oneness.*

*They who by progress have grown from the darkness,*
*Lifted themselves from the night into light,*
*Free are they made from the Halls of Amenti,*
*Free of the Flower of Light and of Life.*
*Guided they then, by wisdom and knowledge,*
*Passes from human to the master of Life.*

*There they may dwell as one with the Masters,*
*Free from the bonds of the darkness of night.*
—EXCERPT FROM TABLET II OF THE
EMERALD TABLETS OF THOTH

*See ye not that in Earth's heart*
*Is the balance of all things that exist*
*And have been on its face?*
*The source of thy Spirit is drawn from the Earth's heart,*
*For in thy form thou are one with the Earth.*

*When thou hast learned to hold thine own balance,*
*Then shalt thou draw on the balance of Earth.*
*Exist then shalt thou while Earth is existing,*
*Changing in form, only when Earth too, shalt change:*
*Tasting not of death, but one with this planet,*
*Holding thy form till all pass away.*

— EXCERPT FROM TABLET XIII OF THE
EMERALD TABLETS OF THOTH

(The above letter was sent anonymously.)

*Dear Spirit of Ma'at,*

*A human being is an encapsulated expression of a much greater, non-physical being with expanded awareness. Ascension is, I believe, a term that describes how human beings are discovering their connection to their greater, or higher, self.*

*As individual human beings choose to recognize their inherent divinity, this increases the overall planetary vibration, leading to higher energy states, which in turn affects the consciousness of others and the Earth herself. As awareness of the spiritual increases in scope, beliefs associated with the old attractor, with its outdated paradigm of competition, conflict, and "follow-the-leader," rise to the surface and are re-examined, leading to the sort of conflict we see in international finance and politics today. This chaotic situation is a necessary precursor to a realignment of thought on a new (and higher) vibrational plateau for mankind.*

*Ascension describes the process of cleansing the species consciousness and releasing embedded beliefs left over from the end of the last planetary cycle. Ascension is the asking for alignment of thought and action with Spirit, which then changes the neurological and physical structure of our bodies.*

*I don't believe there is anything mysterious about ascension. It is a natural and logical outgrowth of mankind's desire for positive change and the operation of universal principles like the Law of Vibration and the Law of Attraction.*

☺ *Ken McLean*

---

*Dear Spirit of Ma'at,*

*Thank you for the invitation to write about my thoughts on ascension. It caused me to wonder for a few moments and then I thought I would share what I am doing at present, sweetly guided by heart energy.*

*I had been living in the high arctic region of Old Crow, Yukon (in 2006) where things began*

to happen that took me deeper into my being than I'd ever been before. Whatever part of me had been resisting the so-called "unknown" let go enough to send me all the way to Edmonton, Alberta, where I ended up attending regular meetings with a master teacher ( John de Ruiter) in a building that is an actual energy vortex (designed according to the Golden Mean and sacred geometry).

The deepening in me continued, and I found myself re-reading the Flower of Life books and the Emerald Tablets, and doing the Earth-Sky Meditation. [The Earth-Sky Meditation is also known as the Unity Breath.] My ability to "see" energy fields and multi-dimensional aspects of life began to open quickly, and I sensed the presence of the Ancients within and around me . . . and that's when I began to understand more about ascension.

To me, ascension is the awakening to authenticity . . . what I truly am . . . and what I was before I arrived here. Things that I was afraid to talk about before (such as the "seeing") are now a natural part of my life, and my heart has gradually opened to a very lovely flow of energy. Instead of thinking of endings and beginnings, I'm observing that I'm in the midst of "expanding" into something greater . . . a greater "Me" so to speak.

For so many years when I talked about oneness and one spirit in all things, I believed I knew what it meant. (One never knows until a shift occurs what the difference is between believing something and truly experiencing it.)

At this point, I have an awareness of the aliveness of everything around me, a knowing about the delicate nature of all life (thanks to everything that has brought me to this point, including dear ones such as Drunvalo, the Kogi, and John). When I walk past a tree with an open loving heart and I feel the tree communicating with me, it's so lovely that my eyes get teary. This kind of awareness causes me to be more gentle in my daily life, more patient, compassionate, and more willing to stay focused on the light, knowing that I'm affecting everything in creation.

I now understand that because of an old ingrained patterning, I had not been totally willing to open every aspect of my being to truth. Trust lives in all of me now, and at this time of ascension, it feels like there is an open door, and a "greater being-ness" lovingly beckoning to the authentic nature in me, to step through and be what I truly am again.

I like the line from the movie Phenomenon, where John Travolta's character (George) said: "Everything's on its way to somewhere." I believe that surrendering to the part of my heart that "knows," assists me with moving forward and upward . . . and I know that each time one of us evolves more, all of us benefit from it. All of us are going together. We truly are One Spirit.

*Much love from my heart to yours,*
*Harmony,*
*"Ti Tika—Tu Toa—Kia Manawa Nui"*
*"Stand True, Stand Strong, Be of Big Heart"*

*From,*
*Makuini Ruth Tai*
*Esteemed Maori teacher*
*From the Land of Everlasting Light*

*Dear Spirit of Ma'at,*

*How can we really know what ascension is un-*
*less we've experienced it? Are we presently ascending*
*in various stages? (Are we in the forest with the trees*
*yet undefined?) Who is really qualified to say, other*
*than the "Ascended Ones"? Is it a matter of "about to*
*have" the experience, or rather, have we been en-*
*gaged for some time?*

*I certainly can't speak from an Ascended One's*
*perspective! To my recollection, I haven't done this*
*before! Yet others such as Joshua David Stone and his*
*Ascension Series have offered well-delineated perspec-*
*tives as self-proclaimed experts. I've always wondered:*
*if we haven't ascended, how can we really know?*

*My first swim in the ascension pool came in*
*1987, as a violet stream directly from Saint Ger-*
*main. He yanked me out of my slumber and prod-*
*ded me to a "messenger,"* Unveiled Mysteries *and*

Magic Presence *tucked under her arm. Showered with Godfre Ray King's magical hand and heart, the imagery of the "Ascension Chair" and those Ones disappearing in a diamond flash was fantastical and exciting. I've held an open mind and hopeful heart, feeling the acceleration; but so far I haven't found the chamber or the chair!*

*Annalee Skarin, author of* "Ye Are Gods," *gave her own fluid account of ascension and, most practically, some precise steps toward it—Praise, Love, and Gratitude. There does seem to be something to this! When I remain in this vibratory triad, it seems to open a doorway to the primordial chamber. I feel lighter, invincible! Is this ascension at play? Annalee supposedly achieved the great translation; if so, I'm in!*

*The controversial account of Berrenda Fox,[5] some years ago, saturated my curiosity. I can boast ticks in the majority of boxes for the "ascension symptoms"—a relief when I've been feeling over-the-top deranged. Yet, by all accounts, these symptoms could also be relative to a number of maladies and diseases, by the medical model. How do we know these are exclusively symptoms of ascension?*

*Drunvalo—a most respected guide upon the path—brought a timely perspective with his summary of three ways to leave the planet; traditional death, resurrection, and ascension. I know I've got at least one of the options covered—only two to go.*

This brought me to yet another turn on the ascension spiral. Could it be that ascension is non-linear and out of a continuum of time and space, making it elusive and subjective as to one's own experience? If so, I suspect that I've been at it since I "awakened" in consciousness in 1987.

Since then, like the Egyptian initiates, life has been a swim through the crocodile chamber, with so many guides and sign posts along the way, in a return to the shore of who "I AM"! I have experienced an incredible personal evolution this past twenty years. Is this ascension through consciousness? I have increased my vibratory frequency and gone through a vigorous scrubbing and cleansing of my emotional, mental, and physical bodies. Am I now readying for another great leap? Is this what we are all waiting for, having been in this same cauldron of transformation since we came to this dimension?

When a fan is at rest, we can clearly see the blades. But when you turn it on, in the speed of the rotation the blades "disappear"; is this what is happening to those of us who are ready, willing, and prepared?

If anyone notices a blinding flash of light and I am nowhere to be found, could you please send me an email!

Namaste,
Deva

Dear Spirit of Ma'at,

Ascension is foremost on my mind these days. There's a diverse amount of information on the subject out there, so I can only best describe my own experience of it.

I feel a deep kinship with Mother Gaia and all of nature, and when I stay in tune with her, I feel myself surrounded with very high frequencies of love and harmony. To me, it's about a choice that we are being given right now; to continue to live in fear and separateness, or to move up with the energies of the Earth as she ascends to a higher reality of Unity Consciousness. It's very much about staying centered in my heart and trusting the universe.

One thing that's opened up for me through all of this is the realization that I have a wonderful team of guides and angels at my disposal. It's really amazing how easy and effortless life becomes when I remember to ask for their assistance! Ascension to me is about letting go of old, limited ways of seeing things and deliberately tuning in to the loving 4th and 5th Dimensional energies that are all around us now. We simply need to place our focus on them and they become our reality . . .

In Lak'ech (I Am Another You)
Wendy Martin

*Dear Spirit of Ma'at,*

*I don't know if this is "quantifiable" or even the truth; I am not even sure where I get such notions, but my definition of ascension is:*

*The uplifting of humanity through a personal and planetary process that is much like a birthing process; first we have to go through the "labor," where it is difficult and hard and the outcome is not at all assured! After going through this and the birth happens, all the hard work is evident and worthwhile! It seems that as I look deep within my heart and psyche, without judgment, I find those places lurking in the shadows that are not in resonance with truth and light! As I illuminate those places with love and compassion, the light of understanding dawns, and I am lifted up into a higher level or dimension of consciousness and awareness. As there is only ONE, and we are all connected, I do this not only for myself but ALL of humanity, AND Mother Earth, Gaia, Pachamamma! It seems that this process is also a cosmic one, and not really one where we have much choice! We can do it consciously, or kicking and screaming. It seems pre-destined.*

*It seems like the Beatles summed it all up years ago. "All you need is LOVE!" the most powerful force in the universe. I believe this force is coming into its own and will carry us all on a tidal wave into a future of peace and upliftment that most likely surpasses anything I can consciously conceive.*

**The Ascension Letters**

I have had an experiential awareness of jumping backward AND ahead on the time line where I went through the birthing process in reverse, saw the moment of consciousness as a multi-colored Maltese Cross, and then experienced myself as a golden seed pod of light held in the loving arms of the Universe/ Creator and downloaded with such an intense, loving energy, like 660 volts of electricity, I cried through the beauty of its duration of forty-five minutes. What a blessing; and NO, I was NOT on drugs.

It is time for mankind to come out of the dark ages and get over the idea of any separation! No more War, Hate, Poverty, Greed, or Tyranny. NONE OF IT! NO MORE! GONE! I am so ready to be on with bigger and better things! There are a lot of New Agers who say this is a planet of duality and it will always be so. I say, WHY? I don't know, but my bones seem to think not!!

Thanks for the opportunity to express my views. I feel so much better.

In Munay,
Tamara Kordahl

---

Dear Spirit of Ma'at,

This forum provides us with a way to thoughtfully delve into the meaning of ascension. It will hold different meanings for different people based on their *life experiences. For me, ascension is about a subtle, gentle, but unmistakable and clear shift in perception in how I live and in my state of being. It comes spontaneously at scalar wave frequency without a shred of conscious thought. In a nanosecond, something inside sounds, and every subatomic part of my being answers the call and moves toward it. When it happens, I don't know consciously how it happens. Months later, when finally confronted by all the deep changes within and without, I begin to understand what took place and when it first began.*

*One day we're living in what we call our "real" world, doing our professional jobs, maintaining households. Feeding family and pets, running errands, visiting with friends; the next moment, something has shifted and changed. As though a switch was turned on, we come to realize that what was once our world no longer is. Everything is changed. Everything is different. What was once acceptable in that world no longer is. Longtime friends, families, jobs and homes, and even lifestyles can disappear. Things are stripped away as a new structure and form of living forms around us. Clutter is reduced and life is simplified. Everything we are or once were is changed or altered forever. With wisdom and greater clarity, we understand that we are part of something much greater than ourselves. We have become connected to a perpetual source energy that nourishes and graces us.*

*Our interests and our focus shifts as our new life structure forms. In that state of new awareness, new consciousness, and new being-ness, we alter our perceptions of life and the way we want to live it. We no longer see ourselves as singular individuals. Instead we recognize and embrace the consciousness of groups. We begin to resonate to a greater consciousness of togetherness and "All-ness" clearly realizing that we're all involved in this unfolding together.*

*We look for and we see a greater universal plan in place and we come to realize our unique roles with other soul groups in that unfolding plan. We now consciously embrace harmony and peace. We consciously become ambassadors of peace instead of war. We see the order and love of the universal divine, and we consciously reflect that back to one another. We look for the good in all things. We honor ritual, ceremony, and natural cycles, recognizing that we are intimately entwined in the cycles of a greater living organism. We become part of the sweetness of the awakening, consciously knowing we have moved into another state of being. In that awareness, we know there's no going back. We have moved into a new consciousness, a new way of living, fully embracing the joy of becoming part of this new dawn. We are in the flow of becoming the new humans.*

*Jo Mooy*
*Sarasota, Florida*

Dear Spirit of Ma'at,

In our perception, the word ascension refers to the evolutionary journey of the soul through incarnation. Every being living in the world right now is actually in the process of ascension, as the Earth's base operating frequency is rising, activating an expansion of consciousness in all life on Earth as the planet passes through the next phase of its evolutionary journey.

When an individual makes a conscious choice to live by the guidance of the heart (or Higher Self) and commits to seeking the light, love, and truth of the Divine Source, he or she has entered a path of conscious ascension. At this point, one begins to recognize and integrate the universal Laws of creation and manifestation.

The process of ascension has its roots in the ancient Egyptian, Tibetan, and Indian cultures of the eastern hemisphere, and in the Mayan culture of North and South America. According to the Indigenous Elders, who are our teachers and mentors, these roots spread out into hundreds of tribal cultures, shamanic paths, and spiritual methodologies. When followed back to its deepest roots, all ascension paths lead back to the Ancestors, ancient star-beings form Sirius, the Pleiades, Lyra, and Arcturus who have maintained a loving presence in the evolutionary path of Earthly and human consciousness.

From the methods we have been exposed to, it appears that there are some underlying common *landmarks that one experiences on the path of ascension which indicate universal stages of development. When one first enters the path of ascension, one is naturally drawn to heal and regenerate the physical body and consciously raise its frequency. Most ascension paths include methods and techniques that support and accelerate this raising of frequency by making changes in the diet and lifestyle using various methods of cleansing and purification.*

*As one advances on the path of ascension, one experiences a progressive change in one's physical and energy bodies. Gradually, consciousness grows in the chakra system, expanding into the Hara Line (Pranic Tube), then into consecutive levels of the Light Body. Each stage or initiation brings a more conscious connection between the Light Body and the physical body, until the two merge and become One. At this point, one experiences these bodies as one unified light substance, un-separated. As one continues on the path, one harmonizes the personal frequencies and expands into an experience of oneness with the Earth, with God, and with all life, everywhere.*

*In perfect synchronicity with our Earth's planetary ascension, many people are currently awakening to the desire to walk a conscious ascension path. The methods and techniques for ascension that are appearing daily, worldwide, are being offered in response to our human desire as tools to support us in the choice for conscious ascension.*

*Here in our location in Anchorage, Alaska, the word ascension has become an everyday buzz word. The Elders say that it is a positive thing, since the word ascension has a resonance that activates the human heart and cosmic memory and helps to raise the mass consciousness. Though each individual ascension path may appear different than the others, we must remember they are all leading to the same destination. . . .*

*Many blessings to each of you who are walking the path of conscious ascension; May you find love, truth, and fulfillment on your journey.*

*Kathryn and Michael Sharp*

Wow! How about that? Aren't people amazing? What you just read is a sampling from hundreds of letters, any one of which could have been used in this chapter. Hopefully, hearing what these people have to say about their take on the ascension process gives you more of a feeling for it and takes some of the mystery out of it. Ultimately, the answer to the mystery can only be found by going within.

We walk the spiritual path for a lot of different reasons. No matter what it is that moves us to go down that road, over time the desire to *"Know thy self"* evolves beyond the self and into the understanding that we happen to be one with all things; that understanding starts in the mind, but as soon as we experience it directly, it becomes something else altogether. From that point on, we can no longer live as if we are apart from anything because we are conscious of the fact that everything we think and feel and do has an impact on the greater whole.

Right now, the greater whole is going through a process that will culminate with the Earth's ascension into the Fifth World. If we wanted to, we could ignore that fact, keep living our lives the way we always have, and laugh all the way to the pole shift. The laissez-faire approach is as good as any. But if we're inextricably connected to it all, how can we rationalize copping out at a time like this? Knowing what we know, it seems unthinkable. If the spiritual aspect leaves us cold, from a purely practical perspective, common sense tells us that anyone would be stupid not to be prepared for something like this.

As of this writing, we've got about a year to prepare; and even though many of us are of the mind that we can turn this around with the power of thought, it seems a bit arrogant to think that we could pick up a paperback in the self-help section and assume that reading it through would be enough achieve that level of mastery. Try using the power of thought to keep the sun from rising tomorrow; if you can figure out how to do that, then come and talk to me about staving off the pole shift with an affirmation or two.

At the same time, anything is possible. Take the Lights for example. A few thousand people changed the course of history just by re-establishing their connection to what was theirs all along. And based on the hundreds of letters we received, none of them seem to be suffering from apocalyptic fears nor did anyone mention holing up in an underground bunker with a crank radio; if anything they're rejoicing about their lives and happy to be here to be part of this. Turning the Light on doesn't sound like such a bad idea; what if we all did it?

Until the Mamas saw the lights beaming all over the planet, even *they* didn't know that their "Younger Brothers" still had the capacity to open their hearts. Evidently, what is inherent in all humans is alive and well inside each one of us. This means that we still have the ability to wake up enough inside to cushion the blow and lessen the cataclysmic aspect of the pole shift. According to many, the work we've already done has altered things considerably, enough to make this a seventeen instead of a ninety-degree shift.

Ultimately, it is our level of consciousness and the degree to which we are able to hold ourselves in the heart space that will determine how we get through this. Aligning ourselves with the energies that are currently streaming in and attuning ourselves inwardly isn't such a hard thing to do. And perhaps knowing that it makes a difference will inspire us to shift our attention away from our outer preoccupations and consider ourselves an integral part of this phenomenon—enough to realize that everything we are and all of what we do makes a difference right now. On the front lines, here we are, on the cusp of the Great Shift. We've waited thirteen thousand years for this moment; why would anyone not want to be prepared for it?

## CHAPTER II

# Beaming Up

We've covered a lot of ground since we checked out of Sunday school. Can you believe it? All the way from biblical programs and apocalyptic misconceptions that deny all of the possibilities we have discussed, to the realization that underneath it all, the ascension process is about us moving out of ignorance and darkness into an expanded vision of who we are.

Our attempt to understand it has taken us into areas of discussion that are new to many of us and so far beyond the boundaries of belief, I wondered if we might be expecting too much from ourselves; but the limits of belief only prevent us from seeing that life is expanding and so is our consciousness. As much as our conversation has gone over the top, everything we've said makes a lot more sense than what we had on our plate to begin with. Clearing out the confusion, looking at what we're left with, we are now faced with the choice to believe it or not.

If you were to ask me, "What makes you so sure about this?" I'd have to tell you I've been sure about it ever since I was a kid. Cellular memories of Atlantis, combined with an intuitive sense that certain things were due to come to pass in my lifetime, created an inner knowing that has never wavered. Even so, I still question myself because a) I've lived long enough to know that anything can happen, and b) I am just as clear that it never works to try to "be right" about anything.

The last thing I ever wanted to turn into was the New Age version of a Born Again Christian, so before we continue, let me say that it's okay with me if I'm totally wrong about all of this. For all I know, life as we know it could go on just the way it is; maybe all this talk of ascension and pole shifts is just a ruse that keeps the gurus and the purveyors of spiritual paraphernalia in business.

Even if the ancient texts, the timing of universal cycles, the Indigenous prophets, and the scientists are all wrong, most of us are clear that life as we know it cannot, and probably will not, continue as it has. The oceans are dead, the ice caps are melting, our air is full of poison, and our soil is bereft of the minerals that fill us with life. If the thought of ascending into the Fifth World isn't something you can embrace, maybe you're aware enough of what's happening on the planet to know that shifting our consciousness is the only way to heal it. Whether we believe in the imminence of a dimensional shift or we're more willing to accept the idea that humanity needs to change its ways, it doesn't really matter; the truth is, all the things we've talked about are a necessary part of our survival right now.

When the Bible told us about the Last Days, it put the emphasis on the coming of the day of the Lord and the restoration of the Kingdom to Israel. The occultists and the astrologers attach the same connotation to our entrance into the Age of Aquarius. From their perspective, crossing that boundary insures that the Christed being in all men will awaken and pour forth to create two thousand years of peace and harmony. In their turn, the Indigenous Elders tell us that the dimensional shift will mark our entrance into one of the most beautiful worlds in Creation.

If this is where we're headed, apart from our practical questions and concerns, the main issue calls us to recognize that we are the ones who have come to dream this new world into being. When the Indigenous people say, "*we are the ones we have been waiting for,*" they remind us that it won't be the powers that be or some new messiah who will come along and restore peace to this planet; it is *we* who will change the world.

According to the Hermetic Axiom, the very nature of the Great Shift implies that everything about *us* has to shift as well; so before we can even think about dreaming up a new world, we have to change ourselves. At this point, the Eight-Ball seems to be telling us that it's time to leave the outer limits of mechanization and materialism and reverse our perspective on *all of it*, enough to come down to Earth and live from the heart, whether the poles shift or they don't.

Those of us who are in no doubt about either the ascension or the pole shift are probably wondering what more we can do. Keep in mind that the Elders are still coming forward with information, so the question of "what more can we do" can only be answered based on what they have said up until now. If all of the evidence adds up, there are a lot of things we could be doing, but this experience is happening on so many levels, maybe it would be best if we took one thing at a time.

# Getting Real

The first order of business might be to stop and look at where we are in our lives. Where do we place the emphasis? Are we so hooked up to our mechanized reality that we can't disengage from it? Are we so besieged by our debts and our monetary concerns that there's no time for anything but work? When we finally settle down at the end of each day, is there any room for any of the things that we've talked about to enter our thoughts and perhaps fill us with another reason for living? Or are we so depleted from having to manage it all that the spiritual component and any fulfillment we might receive from the natural world are no longer part of the schedule?

As I said before: how much would it take for us to slow down and get real about being human? What could we rearrange? If our goals and ambitions for the future don't factor a dimensional shift into the equation, it might be good to redefine them and consider the extent to which they are even relevant at this point. At rock bottom, if in truth we're a hair's breadth away from a pole shift, our plans for any future we might have on this level of experience would seem to be inconsequential. If you're driving yourself nuts trying to figure out how to pay for your three-year-old's college education, or pushing toward something that only has significance in this reality, you might want to reconsider your Five-Year Plan and try sitting down on the floor and *playing* with your three-year-old instead of worrying about whether you'll be able to cover the tuition to Harvard.

Those of us who are saving up for, or are in the process of building, our dream home need to consider everything we said about "natural materials," because otherwise our investment will come to naught in the face of a pole shift. What I find so interesting about all of this is the thought that we're ascending into a realm where we can "imagine" the dream house and manifest it without pounding one single nail. Seen in that light, maybe we're all better off renting, or making do with the space that we're in, because there seems to be no point in trying to establish anything permanent on a planet that is about to shift into a totally different dimension. If we build anything at all, we can't construct it the way we have in the past.

Everything we aspire to needs to be reviewed. All of our core beliefs, including the ones that we have yet to recognize, prevent us from seeing that all they do is hold us back from any level of joy and fulfillment or any connection to the meaning in our lives. Getting real about being human could require us to abandon thought forms that have come to represent everything to us.

Our customary relationship to the orgasm is a case in point. With what we know about it now, can we see that everything we've been told about that aspect of ourselves needs to be rearranged in order to find any spiritual satisfaction in an experience that has been billed as merely a pleasant physical sensation?

When we realize that everything from our biological drives to our innermost thoughts have been ordered by constructs that deny any affiliation with Spirit, how does the prospect of having to dismantle everything we have been led to believe affect us? This includes the beliefs we hold about family, relationships, work, money, love, marriage, God—all the way down to our purpose for being here. In the wake of recent changes, many of us have already had a taste of what it feels like to have to give up more than one illusion.

If you're wondering why the castle appears to be crumbling, it's because the initial breakdown phase that we talked about in a previous chapter began when the Blue Star appeared; it went into overdrive approximately two years ago. The Elders told us that the comet heralded the beginning of the End Times and that there would be a two-year window during which we would witness the dissolution of the old paradigm. Those of us who've paid attention have undoubtedly noticed that all of the changes that have taken place in the outer world since the autumn of 2007 have engendered an erosion of faith in everything we have come to believe in; everything from the religious systems to the medical establishment, all the way up to the people in power.

If the Blue Star was the harbinger of change, it pulled the rug out from under our *ultimate* illusion less than a year after it was spotted in the sky. By September 2008, all of the financial systems of the world collapsed. In a society that has come to value money over and above all things, the fall of the Money God created a chain reaction that led, in stages, to the dissolution of everything else. As a result, all of our values have been called into question; with their Lord and Master out of commission, they have nothing left to stand on.

When we subtract money from the equation, who are we, really? Minus our expenses and our savings, what do we value and where do we place our worth? What are our real resources? If we bewail the collapse of the markets and all of the changes that have come down in the last two years, did it ever occur to us that there might be a reason for it? According to the Elders, the Golden Calf fell off its pedestal because everything it represents prevents us from recognizing what life really is and who we really are.

At a time when knowing who we really are is the only thing that matters, instead of wondering where the money went, maybe we need to start looking at how much it has kept us from connecting with one another, ourselves, and our purpose for living. Regardless of who engineered the Great Bush Depression, underneath it all, the disappearance of the Money God was meant to open our eyes, not just to life and ourselves but to the idea that everything we held faith in was coming apart at the seams.

That two-year window came to a close at the end of October 2009. If you are reading this book, chances are it is late spring or perhaps the early summer of 2010. Some have predicted that the ascension would be a thing of the past before anyone opened these pages; others told us it was sure to happen in August of 2010, which means that this field guide is either gone with the wind or is about to provide everyone with a down-to-the-wire *Cliff's Notes* for an event that is slated to take place in no time at all. If all of us are still present and accounted for, at this point it might be good to look at how we're going to approach the ascension and consider the reality of the pole shift in more detail.

## Preparations

We've already made it clear that it's time to go within. Whatever that has meant to us in the past, it seems as if we're being called to address it with greater sincerity now. The prophets who tell us "the time has come" have prompted many of us to become more serious about things that haven't required this much attention in a long time. If that is the case, hopefully the Unity Breath, the Heart Process, the Mer-Ka-Ba information, and the Ankhing Practice will reinforce your prayers and open the space for the ascension process to unfold within you, through your wish to understand and experience it to the fullest. The inner focus is the main thing. Beyond that, what can we do to prepare?

The way we prepare will be different for each of us. For some, it may work better to just go along with the flow of our lives, trusting that when the time comes, the Christ codes will awaken and carry us through. Of late, I have come to realize that this approach is as good as any. In a recent conversation with Drunvalo, he indicated that we will know exactly what to do when the Shift begins because the ascension codes are alive inside all of us, waiting to be activated by the changes that occur at the time. According to him, we will be acutely aware that the process has begun and understand exactly how to enter into it.

As much as I know this is true, this is one event I want to be prepared for. It could very well be my over compulsive Virgo tendencies that propel me to go whole hog with my prayers and decrees, but regardless of that, there's something about this experience that would prompt anyone to want to rise to the occasion. Those of you who are more inclined to want to have your dime ready when it's time to get on the bus might benefit from hearing about some of my preparations.

They have included:
- Stabilizing my living situation
- Simplifying everything
- Giving what money I have to people who can use it to get their lives together (This has undone any belief I had about the importance of saving money. Watch what happens when you give it away.)

- Living as if today was the day
- Practicing holding myself in the heart space no matter what's going on (I figure a pole shift is probably the ultimate distraction, and I want to be able to stay centered for the duration.)
- Doing nothing for long periods of time
- Staying in the moment
- Being there for the ones I love
- Seeing God in all life
- Swimming
- Observing my fears, and getting to the bottom of them
- Sun gazing
- Fasting
- Meditating
- Prioritizing; anything that takes me out of joy or out of my heart is not a priority
- Observing and listening to Nature
- Invoking the Ascended Masters
- Doing what I have always wanted to do
- Practicing the presence of God
- Remembering Unity

I have also thought about:
- Building a sustainable pole-shift shelter in my backyard
- Taking advantage of the 2-for-1 offer at the floatation-chamber spa up the street (If the three days of darkness is the ultimate sensory deprivation

chamber, I figure this will give me a good chance to practice.)

- Dropping everything and living life to the fullest as soon as this manuscript is done

The way I see it, if we are the ones we've been waiting for, it is the light in us or who we are in our fullest realization that has to come into being before we can really fill that role. If our daily actions include the spiritual element, doing what we can to enhance our connection to it can only do good. Preparing for the ascension could be a simple matter of opening our hearts to the truth about ourselves, knowing that, ultimately, it is the light in us that will carry us into the next world.

## What about Our Nearest and Dearest?

What will happen to our loved ones is a good question; I've thought about it for years. One of my main goals in life has always been to create a sustainable nest, big enough to house everyone in my family. I thought this would be the best way to keep them all safe, but I was wrong. Over time, I've gotten pretty clear about the fact that each of us will go through the ascension process on our own; you, your partner, your children, your pets—everyone passes through the Great Void alone.

For the past five years, I've lived three thousand miles away from my children. Thoughts about their safety during the pole shift troubled me beyond belief, until I realized that everyone makes it to the other side one way or another. Between the ascension codes and the resurrection codes that were firmly installed by Christ two thousand years ago, when his Spirit pours forth, all of us will either die and be reborn or ascend to the next level. When we arrive in the Fifth World, all we have to do is think about our children or any of our friends and loved ones, and they will be there. (I suspect even Elvis would show up if you thought about him, so you can be sure Fido and Fluffy will be there too.)

## Minor Details

I wouldn't bother to pack a lunch. I have a feeling our bodily needs and functions will be suspended when the dimensions shift. Water may be necessary, but who knows? What sustains us here isn't what keeps us alive in the next world, and I'm pretty sure Jesus didn't bring a sandwich when he disappeared into a cloud; food and water could be nothing more than extra baggage where we're going. If you decide to build a pole-shift shelter, you could always stock it with water and dried fruit or nuts and maybe throw in a chamber pot just in case, but I have a feeling that our bodies will adjust to this frequency shift in ways that make their 3D requirements a non-issue as soon as the process begins.

Which brings up another big question: who knows where we'll be when the six-hour window opens up?

We could be twenty hours from home, waiting in an airport on another continent. We might be sitting in a traffic jam listening to the radio, on a subway heading from Manhattan to the Bronx, or at the supermarket picking up a few groceries; we could be anywhere when the ascension portal opens up.

Wherever we are, we'll have to figure out how to stay centered enough to remember what to do, knowing that what we have been waiting for is about to unfold, and remain as open to the experience as we possibly can. No matter where that is, when the ascension begins, the advice of the Taos Elders is simple and sound: *"Go into the 'Pueblo,' close the curtains, don't look outside, and pray."* For us, the "Pueblo" will be wherever we happen to be.

Fortunately, none of us will be in danger because the body is the ultimate Pueblo. When we close the curtains of our eyes and enter the unity of the heart space, we are tuned to Christ Consciousness. That level is the one we are ascending to. When we are in alignment with that frequency, the codes that were seeded so long ago automatically become activated through the law of resonance. If we are not on that bandwidth, chances are we will be subject to too many fears to ride out the pole shift in one piece.

I say this because as soon as the six-hour phase begins, our memories start to dissemble. The feeling that we are losing our minds, along with the inability to stay centered, generates panic; panic breeds fear, fear builds on itself, and as it escalates, we manifest whatever we're thinking and feeling. If we're in a crowd, surrounded by others who are afraid and out of control, the sense of chaos multiplies. As we mentioned in an earlier chapter, many people die during this phase of the pole shift because it's very easy for our fears and/or other people's fears to get the best of us. This is why it's so important to inform ourselves and be inwardly prepared, because the fear issue is a crucial one, both before and after the Shift.

It has been said that love and fear are the two primary emotions on this planet. Every other feeling state falls into one category or another. If we remember that the Third Dimension is governed by the Law of Polarity, we begin to see that like light and darkness, love and fear are just opposite ends of the same pole.

In a universe where love is the fundamental principle and unity is the operative word, fear is an aberration that keeps us apart from the truth. Ascending out of polarity, addressing the extent to which our fear and lack of trust interfere with our ability to experience any sense of love and oneness, is a big item. Don't be afraid to look at it, and don't be afraid to make changes that allow you to deepen your connection to your inner life. The minute we turn up the dimmer switch and enlighten the forgotten aspect of our consciousness, fear and ignorance evaporate and the heart opens to the love and light that fills us all.

# Is This Really It?

A few days before I finished this manuscript, out of curiosity I asked Drunvalo if there was any chance all of this might be called off by the archangels, the Ascended Masters, or any of the other legions of dwellers and beings who inhabit the spiritual realms. His answer was "*No*"—and he went on to say, "*Mother Earth wants this. Nothing can stop it.*"

So here we stand on the ascension threshold, waiting to make our entrance into a whole new world, wondering how to end a conversation that hasn't even begun. If we've gone into it as far as we can, hopefully this field guide will serve as a springboard that takes us deeper into the mystery. As we continue, what can we envision? Or is it even possible to envision the next dimension with Third Dimensional eyes? Perhaps it's enough to know that we're finally going home and that all of our questions will be answered upon our return.

Until then, inform yourself, take time to slow down, and come to terms with your life and yourself. Think about everything we've said. All the things that make it seem as if we are in peril are illusory. Let your fears give way to the understanding that it is a sacred thing to be present at this birth and that each one of our Souls came here to be part of it. The heart is the key. If we do what we can to bring our hearts to this experience, our translation into Spirit will be a joyful and ecstatic rebirth for all of us and for Mother Earth as well:

You ask, what can we do here on Earth that will prepare us for this experience of the higher worlds?

It's definitely not collecting food and making a hole in the ground or anything else like that. Not that this is a wrong action, only that physical preparation has its limits. In heaven, in the higher worlds, you are what you create. It is true here too, but most of us don't know it. From the Fourth Dimension on, it becomes obvious.

Since we are what we create, then it becomes important and necessary that our emissions are in harmony with all life everywhere. We come to understand that everything we think, feel, and do creates the world we must live in. Therefore, ordinary life here on Earth can be seen as a school, a place where each moment of life gives us lessons that can be directly translated into the next world. No wonder Egypt and most of the ancient civilizations regarded death with such reverence. Death, no matter how it comes, is the doorway of darkness into the Void that leads into the brilliant light of the higher worlds of life. If mastered, it leads directly into a conscious connection with all life everywhere—eternal life!

So what about these earthly lessons? The truth is that the Source of all life is in the eyes of every person created. So even here on Earth, great intelligence and wisdom and love are present in every moment inside each person. Once this is seen, then it becomes clear that your thoughts, feelings, and actions are the key. You know exactly what to do. In simple words, it's perfecting your character. The shining diamonds in your character become the survival tools of ascension.

Buddha, Mother Mary, Lao-Tzu, Mohammed, Jesus, Abraham, Krishna, Babaji, Sister Teresa, and about 8,000 other great masters of the eternal light—these are your schoolteachers and the heroes of life. By their example, they show you how to build your character. All of them feel that loving your neighbor is the key. It brings order into the world you create. It gives you eternal life. Do you see? . . .

Life in the next world will seem normal and ordinary once growth begins. You will have entered one of the three highest overtones of the fourth dimension—the tenth, eleventh, and twelfth overtones. In one or more of these three worlds you will gain the knowledge and wisdom to move into the fifth dimension, the beginning of a return trip straight back to God, ever changing as the truth unfolds.

The eyes of the universe are upon us, the great souls of the universe are watching us closely. We are the children of God who offer the possibility of new life.[1]

# Endnotes

## Chapter 1

1. John 20:1–2, *New American Standard Bible* (Philadelphia and New York: A. J. Holman Company, 1977).
2. John 20:12–18, *New American Standard Bible.*
3. Acts 1:3–5, *New American Standard Bible.*
4. Acts 1:6–11, *New American Standard Bible.*
5. Acts 2:1–4, *New American Standard Bible.*

## Chapter 2

1. Acts 1:7–8, *New American Standard Bible.*
2. Acts 2:17–21, *New American Standard Bible.*
3. 2 Peter 3:8, *New American Standard Bible.*
4. Levi, *The Aquarian Gospel of Jesus the Christ* (Marina del Rey, CA: DeVorss & Company, 1907), chapter 175, verses 24–30, pp. 251–252.
5. Lynn Pinknett, *Mary Magdalene: Christianity's Hidden Goddess* (New York: Carroll & Graf, 2003), 83–84.
6. Ibid., 76–77.
7. Michael Baigent, Richard Leigh, and Henry Lincoln, *Holy Blood, Holy Grail* (New York: Dell, 1983), 400.

## Chapter 3

1. William Q. Judge, *The Ocean of Theosophy* (Los Angeles, CA: United Lodge of Theosophists, 1922), 3–4.
2. *Time Magazine, http://en.wikipedia.org/wiki/Time_Magazine,* August 4, 1952.
3. All the details around the story of Merlin can be found on Drunvalo Melchizedek's DVD, *The Story of England.* The Vesica Pisces is the universal symbol for the Divine Feminine.
4. Samuel W. Taylor, "The Puzzle of Annalee Skarin: Was She Translated Correctly?" *http://members.tripod.com/robtshepherd/annalee-skarin.html.*

5. Li Po, *Ascended Master Dictations 2: Talks with the Masters* (Bloomington, Indiana: Author House, 2004), 2–3.

## Chapter 5

1. Luke 21:25–28, *The Jerusalem Bible* (New York: Doubleday Press, 1966).
2. Drunvalo Melchizedek, *The Ancient Secret of the Flower of Life: Volume II* (Flagstaff, Arizona: Light Technology Publishers, 2000), 432.
3. The instructions for the Mer-Ka-Ba Meditation can be found in chapter 13 of *The Ancient Secret of the Flower of Life: Volume II* by Drunvalo Melchizedek.
4. Melchizedek, *The Ancient Secret of the Flower of Life*, 436.
5. Ibid.
6. Ibid., 437.
7. Ibid.
8. Ibid., 435.

## Chapter 6

1. Melchizedek, *The Ancient Secret of the Flower of Life*, 437–438.
2. In *Rabbinic* traditions, Metatron is the highest of the *angels* and serves as the celestial scribe. It has been said that Enoch became Metatron after he made his ascension. Others connect Metatron with Yeshua, or Christ.
3. Excerpted from a channeling that came through Carolyn Evers in June 2009. Carolyn's work can be found at *www.carolynevers.com* and *www.metatronminutes.com*.
4. Melchizedek, *The Ancient Secret of the Flower of Life*, 438–439.
5. Robert Pettit, PhD, *You Can Avoid Physical Death: Physical Body Ascension to the New Earth* (New York: iUniverse, Inc., 2009), 224.

6. Excerpted from a channeling that came through Carolyn Evers in June 2009. Carolyn's work can be found at *www.carolynevers.com* and *www.metatronminutes.com*.

7. Melchizedek, *The Ancient Secret of the Flower of Life*, 439–440.

8. Revelation 7:1–8, *The Jerusalem Bible*.

9. Patricia Diane Cota-Robles, excerpted from an essay entitled "The Divine Plan Is Unfolding Step by Step" (July 2009). Patricia is a Lightworker, well known in the spiritual community for her inspirational writing. Her work can be found at *www.eraofpeace.org*.

## Chapter 7

1. Drunvalo Melchizedek, *Living in the Heart* (Flagstaff, Arizona: Light Technology Publishers, 2003), 1–2.

2. Ibid.

3. The Blue School Teachings form a body of female wisdom that is four thousand years old. Passed down through lineage descent, those teachings are now being disseminated by Catherine Schainberg in her workshops and at the School of Images in New York City. A disciple of Ms. Schainberg's for more than twenty years, Claudette Melchizedek is known all over the world as one of the best instructors in this method of spiritual development.

4. Choosing to enter the heart with the Male or the Female approach is up to the individual and does not imply that men are limited to the Male way and women are limited to the Female way. Either way works for either sex—and the way one enters the heart is always subject to what the heart calls you to do.

5. Frank Coppieters, PhD, *Handbook for the Evolving Heart* (Marina del Rey, CA: Conflux Press, 2006), 41.

## Chapter 8

1. G. I. Gurdjieff, *All and Everything: Beelzebub's Tales to His Grandson* (New York: Penguin Group, 1999), 924–925.

2. The full instructions for the Mer-Ka-Ba Meditation are included in *The Ancient Secret of the Flower of Life: Volume II* by Drunvalo Melchizedek. Instructors in this method can also be found at *www.floweroflife.com*.

3. Melchizedek, *The Ancient Secret of the Flower of Life*, 4–5.

## Chapter 9

1. Drunvalo Melchizedek, "Ancient Egyptian Sexual Ankhing," *Spirit of Ma'at* 1, no. 9 (April 2001). Also see the *Spirit of Ma'at* magazine archives at *www.spiritofmaat.com*.

2. Ibid.

3. Ibid.

## Chapter 10

1. For more information about the super psychic children, the reader is referred to the book *China's Super Psychics*, by Paul Dong and Thomas Raffill (Marlowe and Company, October 1997).

2. Melchizedek, *Living in the Heart*, 48.

3. Ibid., 49.

4. Ibid.

5. Berrenda Fox is an authority on the DNA changes that are taking place as part of our preparation for the ascension process. She believes that in adapting to those changes, the body manifests various physical symptoms.

## Chapter 11

1. Melchizedek, *The Ancient Secret of the Flower of Life*, 440–441.

# Glossary

**Akashic Records** — the etheric records that hold the imprint of everything that ever was, is, or will be. They are said to contain all knowledge of human experience and the history of the cosmos and as such could be considered the "Mind of God."

**Ascended Masters** — individuals once incarnated on the Earth plane who mastered their life lessons by fulfilling their Dharma (life purpose) and burning off at least 51 percent of their negative Karma. Also known as Mahatmas, Elder Brothers, the Great White Brotherhood, and/or the Masters of Wisdom.

**Ascension Codes** — a reference to the codes that were installed in the Akashic Records when Christ made his ascension. They were also etched into the collective DNA through the bloodline that issued out of the union between Christ and Mary Magdalene.

**Baba Ram Dass** — a contemporary spiritual teacher who wrote the 1971 bestseller *Remember Be Here Now*.

**Babaji** — Babaji, or "Mahavatar Babaji" (meaning great avatar/revered father), is said to have been Krishna in a former life. At this point in time Babaji is in direct communion with Christ. Working together, their efforts go into inspiring humanity to turn away from concepts of war, greed, and separation. No one knows the details of Babaji's age or birth. Reputed to be ageless, Babaji was said to be over 500 years old in accounts from the 1800s.

**Bloch Wall** — the point in any electromagnetic domain where the polarities change, or rotate, allowing north to become south and south to become north.

**Blue Star** — otherwise known as "Comet Holmes," the Blue Star appeared in the heavens on October 26, 2007. Blue in color, the comet was gaseous in nature and grew to be bigger than the sun. If astronomers were astounded by this anomalous celestial body, to the Hopi Elders the arrival of the Blue Star marked the fulfillment of an ancient prophecy; one which stated that the Blue Star's appearance would herald our entrance into the Fifth World.

**Christ Codes** — the codes for resurrection, ascension, and reincarnation that were installed in the collective unconscious by Jesus Christ during his time on Earth.

**Christ Consciousness** — the state of consciousness in which the Soul embodies the highest human potential and exemplifies all of the qualities that we attribute to Jesus Christ. In aspiring to attain Christ Consciousness, the application of spiritual values in daily life is the key that awakens our ability to access that aspect of our Being.

**Chohan of the Seventh Ray** — term referring to Saint Germain as the chairman of the committee of Masters who have been elected to superintend our passage through the Great Shift (*see also* God of Freedom for the Earth and Hierarch of the Age of Aquarius).

**Djwhal Khul** — a Tibetan Master in the tradition of ancient esoteric spirituality; he is one of the Masters of the Ancient Wisdom. Said to have incarnated as Caspar, (One of the Three Wise Men who foresaw the birth of Christ), Djwhal Khul serves as the "communications director" for the Ascended Masters. According to Alice Bailey, he prefers to be regarded as a teacher and not as an object of devotion.

**Eckhart Tolle** — a German-born spiritual teacher and the author of the bestselling books *The Power of Now* and *A New Earth*.

**Elder Brothers** — *see* Ascended Masters. Aside from being a reference to the Ascended Masters, it should be noted that the Kogi Mamos also refer to themselves as our "Elder Brothers."

**Enoch** — the Great-Grandfather of Noah, Enoch entered the Melkizedek priesthood at the age of 25 and translated into Spirit when he was 430 years old. The Mormons believe that he founded the city of Zion. In other traditions Enoch was seen as a prophet and a man of patience and truth. Upon his Ascension, he was taken into heaven and awarded the position of the "Great Scribe." Some sources say that Enoch became Metatron after he ascended; others believe that Metatron is connected with Yeshua, or Christ.

**Eye of the Needle** — the "Eye of the Needle" is a metaphor for the portal to heaven. Taken from the Book of Matthew, the phrase comes from a passage which states: *"It is easier for a camel to fit through the eye of a needle than it is for a rich man to enter the Kingdom of Heaven."*

**Female Light** — the Female Light is another term for the Goddess energies that are being reawakened as we leave the dark half of the Grand Cycle and open our hearts to the feminine wisdom that is intrinsic to the Age of Light.

**Fifth Sun** — this refers to the Fifth World, also known as the Time of the Fifth Sun. Indigenous wisdom tells us that the Fifth Sun shines down on one of the most beautiful worlds in creation. (*see* Fifth World).

**Fifth World** — the next stage of Earth's evolution; the ascension of the planet and its inhabitants.

The Indigenous spiritual traditions tell us that the Fifth World is where we will be after we make our Ascension. According to those teachings, it is a place where everything in creation coexists in a state of unconditional love and oneness.

**Fourth Dimension** — the dimension we'll be in once we complete our ascension.

**God of Freedom for the Earth** — term referring to Saint Germain as the chairman of the committee of Masters who have been elected to superintend our passage through the Great Shift (*see also* Chohan of the Seventh Ray and Hierarch of the Age of Aquarius).

**Grand Cycle** — an approximately twenty-six-thousand-year cycle during which the solar system moves in and out of the light generated by the galactic center. In astronomical parlance, the Grand Cycle is another term for the Precession of the Equinox.

**Great Shift of the Ages** — this is the term for the point in the precession cycle at which our solar system moves out of the darkness into the light. The Great Shift of the Ages is always attended by a consciousness shift that is reflected at the physical level as a shifting of the Earth's polar axis.

**Great Void** — the empty, dark space that separates one dimension from another. Akin to "the waters of the deep" referred to in the first chapter of Genesis, the Great Void is the Womb of Creation. It is out of this space of emptiness or nothingness that all life emerges and is changed and renewed in cycles.

**Great White Brotherhood** — *see* Ascended Masters.

**Hermetic Axiom** — This refers to a universal law which states that the macrocosm is reflected in the microcosm, or "As Above, So Below." In the Christian traditions this concept is stated as: "On Earth as it is in Heaven."

**Hierarch of the Age of Aquarius** — term referring to Saint Germain as the chairman of the committee of Masters who have been elected to superintend our passage through the Great Shift (*see also* Chohan of the Seventh Ray and God of Freedom for the Earth).

**Hilarion** — considered to be the Chohan (Guardian) of the Fifth Ray, and one of the Masters of the Ancient Wisdom. Hilarion is here now helping to bring in the scientific aspect of the New Age. His purpose involves teaching us to use our mental powers for the greater good. The guardian of inventors, researchers, and anyone who works to apply spiritual values in the realm of discovery, Hilarion is said to have incarnated as the Apostle Paul. He works directly with the Archangel Raphael.

**Hundredth Monkey Factor**—this is a reference to the Hundredth Monkey Theory which states: whenever a new behavior or thought form is introduced into a population, there is a moment in time when that understanding spreads far enough into a segment of the population to reach what is known as "critical mass." This is defined as the tipping point at which the behavior or thought pattern is automatically and simultaneously transmitted into the consciousness of the population as a whole.

**Kogi**—a Mayan tribe that survived the Spanish invasions by retreating into the highest reaches of northern Colombia's Sierra Nevada mountain range.

**Kogi Mamos**—the spiritual leaders of the Kogi tribe, the Kogi Mamos are the descendents of the High Priests of Atlantis, otherwise known as the Naccal Brotherhood.

**Kundalini**—the term for the Serpent Power, or concentrated life-force energy that lives at the base of the human spine. Awakened through the application of certain spiritual practices, when the Kundalini rises it produces and expanded state of consciousness that is characterized by pure knowledge, pure joy, and pure love. When referring to the planet Earth, the Kundalini is another term for the Serpent of Light, or the spiritual aspect of her polar axis.

**Kuthumi**—one of the members of the Spiritual Hierarchy that oversees the development of the human race on this planet to higher levels of consciousness; a Master of the Ancient Wisdom also known as Koot Hoomi or Master K.H. As the Master of the Second Ray of Wisdom, it was Kuthumi who provided the information for Madame Blavatsky's *Secret Doctrine* and *Isis Unveiled*. A.P. Sinnet's *Mahatma Letters* is another book that owes much of its content to this amazing entity. Said to have been Pythagoras in a former life, Kuthumi has also incarnated as: Pharaoh Thutmose III, Balthazar of the Three Wise Men, Saint Francis of Assisi, and Shah Jahan.

**Kwan Yin**—in the Far Eastern spiritual traditions Kwan Yin is known as the Goddess of Mercy and Compassion.

**Law of Polarity**—according to The Kybalion, the Law of Polarity states: "Everything is dual; everything has poles; everything has its pair of opposites; like and unlike are the same; opposites are identical in nature but different in degree; extremes meet; all truths are but half truths; all paradoxes may be reconciled."

**Law of Resonance** — according to the Law of Resonance anything that vibrates at the same frequency goes into a state of resonance that automatically connects or unites two or more things coherently and simultaneously. This means that everything is harmonically connected. In simple terms the Law of Resonance could be restated as: "like attracts like."

**Lao-Tzu** — a philosopher of ancient China and a central figure in Taoism.

**Mahatmas** — *see* Ascended Masters.

**Master Morya** — Madame Blavatsky's favorite master and teacher, Master Morya is reputed to be the most fiery and candid of all of the Elder Brothers. It was he who provided the plan for *The Secret Doctrine* and *Isis Unveiled*. Highly respected by all of the members of the Great White Brotherhood, Master Morya is deeply attuned to human affairs. He is said to have incarnated as: the Emperor of Atlantis, Abraham, Melchior (One of the Three Wise Men), King Arthur, Thomas Beckett, Thomas More, Akbar, (a Mogul emperor) and as Chandragupta Maurya, the first emperor of India.

**Masters of Wisdom** — *see* Ascended Masters.

**Mer-Ka-Ba** — also known as the Light Body or the ascension vehicle, it is the name for the star tetrahedronal energy field that surrounds the human body. It is universally understood to be the geometric blueprint that allows Spirit to both contain itself in a form and move freely between dimensions.

**New Age Movement** — a decentralized Western social and spiritual movement that seeks "Universal Truth" and the attainment of the highest individual human potential.

**One Heart** — this is a reference to the One Heart that lives and breathes and moves through everything. (*see also* Unity Consciousness).

**Prana** — Hindu word for concentrated life-force energy.

**Pole Shift** — an occurrence during which the Earth's polar axis shifts to align itself with a new star. Pole shifts are a natural part of the Earth's evolutionary process; they occur approximately every thirteen thousand years.

**Serapis Bey** — an Ascended Master and member of the Great White Brotherhood, he is regarded in Theosophy as one of the Masters of the Ancient Wisdom. Known as the Chohan (Guardian) of the Fourth Ray of purity, harmony, and discipline, Serapis Bey was an Atlantean High Priest who migrated to Egypt after the Fall. A series of earthly incarnations as Amenhotep III, King Leonidas, and Phidias (The famous sculptor) led to his Ascension in the year 400 BC.

**Serpent of Light** — the Serpent of Light is another name for the Kundalini of the Earth. (*see* Kundalini).

**Seven Rays** — seven metaphysical principles that govern both individual souls and the unfolding of each astrological age.

**Seven Turn Labyrinth** — a Seven Turn Labyrinth is a unicursal maze that is a symbolic representation of the pathway to enlightenment. In walking the circuits of a Seven Turn Labyrinth the spiritual seeker automatically becomes more centered and whole. Found inlayed in the floors of all the great cathedrals, or carved in miniature at their entryways, walking, or tracing the finger over the turns of a Labyrinth offers members of the congregation an opportunity to go deeper into themselves prior to entering the church.

**Seventh Ray** — holds rulership over the Aquarian Age (*see* Seven Rays).

**Third Dimension** — the dimension in which we all currently live; also called the Fourth World.

**Three Days of Darkness** — the period of time that is spent within the Great Void after the pole shift but before complete ascension.

**Unity Consciousness** — the level of consciousness in which all things are connected in a state of love and oneness.

**Zero Point** — in any magnetic domain Zero Point is the point at which polarity ceases to exist.

# About the Author

Photograph © Demmie Todd

Cal Garrison is a practicing astrologer with 40 years of experience. At present, she goes between casting horoscopes, writing books, and working as the personal assistant to Drunvalo and Claudette Melchizedek. Editor in Chief for the online magazine, *The Spirit of Ma'at,* Cal is also a syndicated columnist for the Associated Press. She has written five books, including *Slim Spurling's Universe: Ancient Knowledge Rediscovered to Restore the Health of the Environment,* and *Mankind and The Astrology of 2012 and Beyond.* Ms. Garrison lives happily in the Red Rocks of Sedona, Arizona.

# The Weiser Field Guide Series

For more than fifty years, Weiser Books has published works for seekers and spiritual practitioners from a variety of traditions, from new consciousness to magick to coming earth changes to Western Mystery, Tarot, Astrology, the paranormal, and more. The Weiser Field Guide series developed out of our desire to introduce a new generation of readers and provide a handbook to esoteric and occult secrets from throughout time and around the world and beyond. We hope these guides entertain and inform.

## IN THE SERIES:

*The Weiser Field Guide to Ghosts: Apparitions, Spirits, Spectral Lights, and Other Hauntings of History and Legend*

*The Weiser Field Guide to Vampires: Legends, Practices, and Encounters Old and New*

*The Weiser Field Guide to Cryptozoology: Werewolves, Dragons, Skyfish, Lizard Men, and Other Fascinating Creatures Real and Mysterious*

## WATCH FOR FORTHCOMING TITLES:

*The Weiser Field Guide to Witches*

*The Weiser Field Guide to the Paranormal*